PRIVATE PARIS

TEXT BY

Marie-France Boyer

PHOTOGRAPHS BY

Philippe Girardeau

PRIVATE PARIS
The Most Beautiful Apartments

PUBLISHERS  NEW YORK

ACKNOWLEDGMENTS

The author thanks above all those who were kind enough
to open their doors to her, as well as the doors of their friends.

She also thanks:
Andrée Putman
Christiane Germain
France Grand
Daphne de Saint-Sauveur
Fabienne de Seze
Elisabeth Garrouste
Denise Durand-Ruel
Emmie de Mortelaere
Jef Gravis
Anne de Fayer
Genevieve Jurgensen
Françoise Teynac

for their enlightening ideas,
their encouragement, and
their friendly advice.

Design
Henri Latzarus

Photocomposition
Bussiere, Paris

Photogravure
Actual a Bienne, Switzerland

Binding
A.G.M. Forges-Les-Eaux

© 1988 Sté Nlle des Editions du Chêne.
Originally published as *Habiter Paris*; text by Marie-France
Boyer, photographs by Philippe Girardeau. Translated from
the French by Anthony Roberts.

First American Edition

Library of Congress Cataloging-in-Publication Data
Boyer. Marie-France, 1942–
    Private Paris.
    Translation of: Habiter Paris.
    1. Interior decoration—France—Paris—History
—20th century.   I. Title.
NK2049.P37B6913   1988   728'.0944'361   88-22315
ISBN 0-89659-922-1

Front cover: Salon in the apartment of Manuel Canovas
Back cover: Bedroom in the apartment of Jacques Garcia

CONTENTS

ABOVE *The hall, with its horse prints by Cavendish, is sometimes used as a dining area. Kilims decorate the floor and the Swedish Karl Johan-style mahogany chairs.*
OVERLEAF *In the salon the furniture is draped with Oriental striped fabrics, and gouaches of Vesuvius hang on the walls.*

"*I always remember the purity of the houses in my native Sweden.*" *BIRGITTA FOURET*

The key to this place is light," asserts Birgitta Fouret. Her fifth-floor apartment faces south, but as it is on a corner, it also has windows facing west. From here one can see bell-towers and domes sprouting from a mass of roofs, as far as the Invalides and the Eiffel Tower — a view that is almost incongruous, because in this interior one imagines oneself surrounded by birch woods and frozen lakes. Not surprisingly, Birgitta's childhood was spent in Sweden in curtainless houses, "always fresh, clean and comfortable," she remembers. However, she thinks that the most formative influence on her taste was her time as a student in London, where she worked with the decorator Geoffrey Bennison. It is to Bennison that she attributes her original touch with old fabrics and her penchant for Orientalism. After years as a brilliant New York fashion model, Birgitta launched a new career as a decorator and antique dealer, moving to Paris's XVIIth *arrondissement* with her children and her husband, the publisher Olivier Fouret.

Her shop is called Haga, after a beautiful summer house belonging to King Gustav of Sweden, which greatly influenced her choice of decoration. By contrast, the objects and furniture she has collected in London, Paris and Stockholm are nearly always from the early 19th century, a richly imaginative period during which all Europe copied the Empire and Directoire styles. Russian furniture began to look like imitation Malmaison, and Swedish bentwood consoles and lion-footed chairs might have been made by Thomas Hope. This is just what Birgitta likes, especially since she is not particularly concerned by the origins or history of the things she buys, but follows her own ideal with considerable determination. As a result, the few pieces of furniture in her house are highly original, and the materials from which they are made are given at least as much importance as their forms.

Among other things, Birgitta is fond of the pink-flecked porphyry known as "Alvaden," which was made fashionable by the Swedish royal court in the 18th century. She also

LEFT *Olivier Fouret's library with its garnet-coloured felt walls and Regency scroll desk.*
BELOW LEFT *A detail showing the Cordoba leather on the side of the Louis XVI couch in the library.*
RIGHT *The collection of family photos and 19th-century medallions, in the library surround a 17th-century Flemish landscape.*

collects Medici vases, lamps, candlesticks, mass-produced butter dishes, magnifying glasses and canes; table legs and lampstands made of ivory; Russian and Swedish silver or enamelled mugs; antique bronze elephants, lions and human heads; and the little statuettes of Egyptian slaves known as Reguli, which come in pairs or fours. The *bayadère* plaster fabric of the costumes worn by the statuettes offsets those of the chairs and the other collections: the interplay is continuous. Thus lions reappear on the armrests of chairs, the eagles on the legs of the pedestal table are echoed on porphyry boxes, and elephants in relief emerge from ivory surfaces. In fact, the same thematic furniture, objects, colours and textiles re-occur throughout the four front rooms of Birgitta's home, all of which are served by a long corridor. The children's bedrooms and the kitchen lead off the same corridor and open onto the back courtyard in classic early 20th-century style. For total unity, Birgitta has painted all the walls the same pale apricot-beige colour, with highlights of white and grey on the *boiseries* and mouldings, "for the light effect." The recently-installed floorboards were waxed very black "for strength," and then the reception rooms were rearranged, eliminating the former dining room altogether. "We eat with the children in the kitchen," declares Birgitta. The kitchen itself is blue and white, neat and tasteful in tone. "When I entertain, I set up a buffet in the hall: the hall also doubles as a sewing room. I do a lot of my things myself on

12

which has a cylinder top, dates from the reign of Louis XVI; here she telephones, writes letters, reads her newspaper and drinks her coffee, surrounded by photographs of her family. "I always seem to be sitting here," she says. Olivier Fouret's Regency desk, made of fruitwood marquetry, is placed in the centre of his office, which is full of bookshelves and is upholstered in a fabric of deep Bordeaux red. A painted Louis XVI couch, deliberately oversized, adds the finishing touch to this room, which was designed by Birgitta as a cosy, studious retreat for winter days.

The dark-toned bedroom, with its profusion of very practical closet space, is almost entirely filled by a large four-poster bed draped in wine-coloured cotton, which is deceptively like watered silk. At its head are two English hall chairs which serve as night tables. From this bedroom one can double back to the hall, which in fact is a kind of crossroads for the entire apartment. A collection of canes, a series of horse engravings by Cavendish and a heap of overcoats, hats and shawls make this a living area where the various members of the household often meet during their daily routine, beneath a fine Gobelins tapestry from Olivier's family.

The apartment which Birgitta Fouret has created is representative of a kind of international taste which is exclusive to the 1980's, a blend of Rome in the style of Hubert Robert with nostalgia for some distant utopia in the style of Delacroix.

the sewing machine."
In terms of colour, the Fouret household seems somewhat paradoxical: white cotton and pale canvas compete with the deep reds and golds of Birgitta's striped Oriental fabrics and the dull glow of her kilim chair coverings. She always uses old fabrics, frequently buying them at the Marché Saint-Pierre, a

uniquely Parisian institution that stocks hundreds of tons of remnants or damaged fabrics. "I don't like the idea of using some *dernier cri* fabric and then coming across it in another person's house," she asserts.
Birgitta's salon is a blend of all the features of the apartment. Bathed in sunlight, candlelit in the evenings, this room is

dominated by three "Campagne d'Egypte" pedestal tables. One of these is Swedish, the two others French, with griffins and winged sphinxes. There is also a superb family commode with a porphyry top. All the glazed double doors are open, scaling down the space and giving full play to the light. Each of the two offices has its own massive desk. Birgitta's,

"Once one's lived on the quays of the Seine, one can never live anywhere else again." YVES MARBRIER

14

Marbrier lives in the former apartment of the verger of Notre Dame; this backs onto the cathedral and faces the Seine where it divides at the Ile de la Cité. His four small windows look directly onto the river, with no intervening street or quay; the 19th-century embrasures frame the water surface like paintings by Marquet.

When Marbrier came here, he found a small four-room apartment covered with flowered wallpaper. His architect, Philippe Boisselier, broke up the existing area of 90 square metres to create a clear-cut "carcass" with distinct spaces and slightly varying levels. The absence of doors made it possible to juggle effects within the space. In order to accentuate the choice of sobriety and bareness, the walls were covered with glossy white paint and the wooden flooring was stained black. The only exception was the bathroom, where turquoise *pâte de verre* was sparingly employed. Marbrier decided to use the upper part of the room as a sleeping area, setting apart its most isolated corner

LEFT   *Light filters through the frosted-glass entrance door, producing an interesting play of colours with the Greek bistro chairs and the Roland Roure toy above.*
RIGHT   *The tip of the Ile-Saint-Louis with the Quai aux fleurs and Notre-Dame beyond.*

for eating and working. This layout can be changed in minutes, since the apartment contains no item that is heavy or bulky. The result is a spacious, unified, well-lit living area.

Marbrier is an art director at the Trois Suisses, where he has been instrumental in popularizing the work of Philippe Starck and Andrée Putman. He is also the creator of the Living Tradition company. His home is furnished with creations by Maurer, Aulenti, Marescal, Starck, van der Rohe and Hoffman. His other passion is travel. "I hate to travel without a purpose," he declares. "I try to meet people and work at the same time; I go looking for utilitarian objects that will fit into contemporary interiors without looking ethnic or traditional." Hence the items in his home: a seat from Kenya, an urn from the Yemen, a chair from a Greek bistro and a Japanese bed. Whatever their origin, these objects share the same tones of indigo, leathery brown or waxed wood, which respond to the black and white of the architecture without inviting comment. In any event, the spectacular position of Marbrier's apartment, with its view of bridges, green water and plane trees trailing in the Seine, inevitably seems much more impressive.

ABOVE LEFT *View of the living room, near the windows that look onto the* quai, *showing a 16th-century Ming table beneath three photographs of plants by Blossfeld (taken in 1928), a chair by Philippe Starck, a piece of metal from a wreck and a Gabonese "Fang" mask.*
LEFT *Another view of the living room — the upper end — which also serves as a bedroom; the entrance and dining room are on the right. Armchairs are by Philippe Starck and chairs by Mies van der Rohe.*
RIGHT *The 1952 Prouvé table — on its Indian "Jail Rug" — doubles as a desk and dining table. The chairs are attributed to Hoffman (1906).*

"I come from the provinces, and I like my house to reflect that fact."
MICHELLE HALARD

Michelle and Yves Halard are chair-makers and fabric printers who live on a small street in the quiet Auteuil quarter of Paris. The entrance is on the first floor; instead of going upstairs, one goes down a spiral staircase which leads to a suite of rooms. These open onto a garden by way of a verandah. The house is certainly not conventional. It has no hallways or corridors; visitors find themselves in a pink salon as they enter. "We've always been advocates of comfort and proper proportions," explains Michelle, "but we also do exactly as we please." The salon, which is the principal room in the house, is decorated with a Jouy cretonne print illustrating the La Fontaine fable of the Fox and the Stork. The room is filled in a deliberately unorthodox manner with paintings from various epochs and with old toys of wood and tin. Michelle and Yves are both inveterate enthusiasts of junk shops, even though the 18th-century *canapé* in the room, painted grey and covered with the same La Fontaine pattern, testifies that they know all about the classical, 18th-century use of the fabric. "I've always been very sensitive to the movement and freedom of a design. I never linger on details, and I don't insist that the design be centred on chairs, etc., unlike most upholsterers," explains Yves. According to the Halards, the Fox and Stork motif is shunned by their clients, who think it too "direct," even too "overtly sexual"!

From the salon, three 19th-century style windows overlook thick foliage, the green of which is echoed by the dark tones of the carpet. "When I come back here in the evening," says Michelle, "I'm often too exhausted to go out and look at my garden: what's more, it's usually after dark. But the knowledge that it's there still makes me happy." All the seats are covered with removable slipcovers, because the Halards don't fuss about messy dogs or about children with jam on their fingers. The chairs and fabrics they sell in their shop are named after people and places they love; among these is their old château in France's Berry region to which Michelle, accompanied by her samples and notebooks, often retreats to work. At all events, their Paris home has the charm conferred by much love and use, blended with the slight dishevelment one always finds in a happy household. Michelle, whose head has never been turned by success, sometimes daydreams that her house in Auteuil exists in another place and time.

LEFT AND ABOVE *The verandah projects into the garden and serves as an office and living room. It also houses Yves Halard's collection of trawlers, steamboats and other models.*

18

ABOVE LEFT *The green-and-gold dining room, with its hint of Baroque. A very thick tapestry serves as a tablecloth.*
ABOVE *The salon opens onto the dining room (on the left) and overlooks the garden. It is decorated with* toile de Jouy, *which combines harmoniously with modern fabrics and prints.*
BELOW LEFT *Detail of the salon, showing the traditional 18th-century couch, upholstered in the same Jouy fabric, and the collection of old toys in the background.*

*"One must be able to achieve surprise,
without sacrificing intimacy.
And all one needs for that is inspiration."*
MADELEINE CASTAING

Madame Madeleine Castaing, at the age of 94, is the high priestess of decorating in Paris. Stylish, whimsical, witty, wildly capricious and hard to please, she still directs all her work; and, like Coco Chanel, she couldn't care less that she is endlessly plagiarized.
In 1941, when she opened her first shop as an *antiquaire-décorateur* (terms she detests),

Castaing invented a neo-19th-century look by bringing *passementerie* and mahogany back into favour. She also prompted new interest in the Second Empire style, imported Biedermeyer furniture and successfully blended Regency styles with Russian neo-Classicism. She based her décor on a collection of rare pieces of furniture, which she unearthed at fleamarkets and elsewhere before anyone else became interested in them; on

carpets printed with flowers, leaves or stripes; and on fabrics copied from old documents. No Oriental carpets ("I detest exotica"), no flowers ("It's too awful to watch them die") and no white lampshades: Castaing prefers half-light, curtain loops high on the wall, quilted chairs and plenty of frills.

ABOVE   *Two views of the Rue Jacob.*
LEFT   *The shop on the corner of Rue Jacob and Rue Bonaparte, which Castaing painted black in 1947.*

Her velvety, theatrical style has remained much the same for the last 50 years. Her own homes are decorated in exactly this way: they exude a kind of nostalgic femininity, unique and inimitable. She has lived on Rue Jacob since 1947, and, scattered around the same quarter, she keeps what she calls her *remises*. These are storage flats, full of furniture and cobwebs, which she occasionally visits; all are arranged like theatre sets, awaiting the day when she will come at last to hold the tea parties and literary soirées she talks about as she adjusts the plastic coverings with the end of her cane.

The sombre ground floor premises give the impression of looking into someone's home rather than a shop. This is exactly what Castaing intended — her shop is more like a series of little salons than a place of business. One hardly dares enter: all around are tables encrusted with mother-of-pearl, mahogany screens, ivy-patterned carpets and lampshades the colour of billiard tables. All this is part of the Castaing "look." When questioned, she may acknowledge that Balzac helped create one of the bedrooms with a description in his *Girl with the Golden Eyes*, or even that it owes something to Flaubert's Sanseverina.... The mezzanine is full of memories of Castaing's husband, Marcellin, who died in 1967. She recalls their 50-year love affair, and their shared enthusiasm for the painter Soutine, whose canvases they collected and framed over a period of many years. Today, Madeleine Castaing possesses one of the greatest collections of Soutine's work in the world, including a number of portraits of herself.

ABOVE *In the half-light of the green salon on the first floor aperitifs and a coffee tray are perpetually ready for use.*
RIGHT *The small neo-Gothic dressing room, upholstered in chintz and en suite with the pink bathroom of the mezzanine floor, was decorated in 1947.*

ABOVE *The* salle de jeu, *with playing cards on the table, is full of 19th-century furniture. The damask and the blue-black carpet were designed by Castaing.*
LEFT *In the peacock-blue* salle de jeu *on the first floor, this early 19th-century mahogany chair with copper and enamel inlays is described by its owner as "the prettiest chair I ever saw."*
OVERLEAF *The pink bathroom, which balances the turquoise bedroom of the mezzanine, is decorated like the boudoir of a 19th-century actress.*

They also spent much of their time at Lèves, a country property near Chartres. Hence the *pied-à-terre* over the shop is more like a love nest than a fully-fledged apartment. The ceilings are very low, all sound is deadened by thick carpeting and each of the tiny windows has its own upholstered banquette. The bedroom and bathroom are classic Castaing; the same style occurs over and over in her work, even though the little flat is now abandoned to dust and nostalgia.

The bedroom is the original example of a light watercolour turquoise, now well known as "Castaing green." The bed, covered in pompom-bordered muslin, evokes the practising Catholic of the 1950's, but the sepia-coloured photographs of very handsome men scattered negligently around are reminders that Castaing is also a high priestess of love.

The boudoir-bathroom is pink, in keeping with its owner's readiness to use all the wiles of femininity. Daylight is filtered through light but opaque cotton curtains; the tub and the furniture have clearly been chosen with the same care that other people reserve for their salons. A charming little neo-Gothic dressing room completes the apartments of this remarkable woman.

Since her husband's death, she has lived on the first floor. There are two ways in: one a worn flight of steps from the shop, the other a main staircase leading from a pretty paved courtyard beside the Rue Bonaparte. The apartment is large and elegant, with high ceilings. It consists of three big rooms *en suite*, linked by a long vestibule. The rooms are all interconnecting, and all the doors are permanently open except the last, which leads into Castaing's pink bedroom.

Here, in her huge bed, is where she now spends most of her time. The décor seems frozen, eternally prepared for some kind of festivity to occur. There is an expectant feel about it all, which imparts a heartrending quality in the dining room where the places are always laid, because, as Madame Castaing explains, "it makes me feel better when I come home." On the tables in the peacock-blue *salle de jeu*, the playing cards are spread close to the cold faïence stove; in the main drawing room, the lights are never switched on. It is here, on the first floor, that Soutine's canvases come into their own as an integral part of the Castaing magic. Here, also, she has "dared" (her own word) to imitate the Brighton Pavilion, to blend widely differing styles, and to display some of her marvellous discoveries. Among these is a gigantic painted steel chandelier, which served as a decorative starting point for the *salle de jeu*, to which at the last minute she added an armchair once belonging to Joséphine de Beauharnais, a figure with whom she likes to compare herself. Like Joséphine, Madeleine Castaing is a kind of sorceress; and she considers Malmaison a house she herself might have decorated, because "in addition to its beauty, it possesses a special charm which belongs to the life of its creator."

ABOVE *The Castaings lived in this low-ceilinged turquoise ("Castaing green") bedroom when they were not at Lèves.* RIGHT *Above the fireplace in the bedroom hangs a portrait of Madeleine Castaing by Louise de Vilmorin, with the initials of an admirer on the trompe l'œil panel behind it.*

"People inevitably decorate their houses with personal obsessions."
CHARLOTTE AILLAUD

Charlotte Aillaud's home near the heart of Saint-Germain-des-Prés is among the best-concealed houses in all of Paris. To reach it, one walks under a porch into a courtyard with a paulownia tree in the middle; on the far side is the *hôtel particulier* in which Charlotte and her husband, the architect Emile Aillaud, have lived for the last 30 years. The house is built in an L-shape and backs onto a garden containing large numbers of yew trees, a stone fountain and an abundance of flowers. Birds chirp in the shade of a single horse-chestnut tree: standing here, it is hard to believe that the terraces of the Flore and the Deux-Magots are only a step away.

Charlotte Aillaud is an editor-at-large for the American magazine *Architectural Digest*. She is unconventional, highly intelligent and a long-time member of the jet-set. Her house is a mysterious, secret place. She loves walls in dark colours such as green, bordeaux-red, sea-blue and even black. Ivy frames all the windows, so that the apartment is an extension of the shadows that surround it. Charlotte has understood that light should never be forced into a room. Here, its muted presence produces a grotto-like atmosphere, suggesting the type of imagination that has kept faith with childhood. The person who lives here is clearly a lover of music, opera and theatre, who is quite happy to use lace and candelabras to the point of excess, along with Fortuny fabrics and lush rose-pink taffetas. In a house like this, one is liable to come across bouquets of violets on table corners, lit by overhead chandeliers.

On the ground floor, Charlotte discovered, under six or seven

LEFT *A sheep by François-Xavier Lalanne stands at the dining room entrance, which looks onto the garden.*
RIGHT *The dining room table is laid for a dinner party with Hungarian porcelain, Murano glasses, 18th-century silver gilt cutlery and Tuscan trompe l'œil fruit that seems to have rolled from the plates.*

layers of paint, elegant wall decoration by Percier and Fontaine depicting veiled muses playing with swans. The Rococo 18th-century *boiseries* in the adjacent salon were also discovered under layers of paint. This area, with its dining table, is a remarkable feature of the house.

The first floor is reached by a spiral staircase, which was designed by Emile Aillaud in 1950 and has acquired the status of sculpture. The bedroom is upholstered in navy blue damask velvet; furniture is as sparse here as elsewhere in the house. The overall atmosphere is created by tiny subtle touches. Virtually the

entire space is taken up by a vast four-poster bed *à la Polonaise*, draped with lace and pleated pink buckram. "I've always adored lace," explains Charlotte. "When I was little, I used to see it everywhere, on choirboys, around cakes and on elegant old ladies. Lace has always inspired me."

A gilded Venetian blackamoor stands guard over this fairytale décor, which is tempered by warm reminders of reality in the form of photographs. Finally, the oval mirror hanging between the two green-draped windows looks like the kind one can step right through.

*"You have to take this salon
with a pinch of salt, despite the fact that
I scrupulously followed an inventory
from Mansart's time when I decorated it."*
JACQUES GARCIA

ABOVE   *A small garden in the French style, only a step away from Place des Vosges.*
TOP   *Detail of the salon ceiling, attributed to Le Brun.*
RIGHT   *Mme. Mansart's bedroom adjacent to the red salon, with a Trianon bed by
Jacob and a Riesener desk.*

ABOVE *The cosy, low-ceilinged kitchen-cum-dining room, reconstructed with 18th-century* boiseries *and original Delft tiles.*
RIGHT *Mansart's former office, which has been entirely reconstructed with original* boiseries, *some from the library of Mme. Sophie, the daughter of Louis XV.*
PREVIOUS PAGE *The sumptuous 17th-century ambience of the red salon, with the armchair that once belonged to the Grand Dauphin, Mme. de Mantenon's day-bed, a Boulle desk and Gobelins and Flemish tapestries.*

acques Garcia is a dynamic individual who entertains regularly. As you watch him settling some detail with the florist or the *patissier,* he seems so enthusiastic that one can imagine he is about to sing a Verdi aria.

For Garcia, good parties are like good theatre. His apartment is decorated sumptuously in red, like the Paris Opéra. Garcia's reconstruction of this first floor of the Hôtel de Sagonne is a stylistic *tour de force* by this decorator, who claims to be "in love with the eclecticism and the sheer medley of Versailles." Jules Hardouin Mansart, the first owner, was 28 years old when he began work on this mansion. It took him ten years to complete, partly because, as Louis XIV's chief architect, he was building the Hall of Mirrors, the Grand Trianon and the Dome of the Invalides at the same time. The ceilings, by Mignard and Lebrun, amazed Mansart's contemporaries. Sadly, in the next 200 years the building lost its *boiseries*, statues, doors and floorboards, while the ceilings, originally painted on canvas and plaster, were encased in layers of masonry and woodwork.

Garcia's work has consisted in reestablishing the original spaces and woodwork, replacing floorboards and restoring ceilings to their former splendour. A composition entitled *Les caresses de Junon faites à Jupiter excitent les rires des hommes qui les montrent du doigt à l'Amour* (Juno's caresses bestowed on Jupiter provoke the hilarity of mortals, who draw them to Cupid's attention) again dominates the salon, which was Mansart's formal bedroom and is decorated with period furniture, much of it signed. The chairs used by Garcia's guests number the same as in the original inventory. Garcia maintains that this proves that "they could not have been lined up against the walls, as purists maintain." The Dauphin's armchair, Madame de Montespan's bed and the chairs covered in period damask and velvet are all enhanced with braiding, lace, embroidery and cushions of gold and silver fabric. The furniture is inlaid, while the walls are covered in Flemish tapestries, dating from 1680, which represent the months. The floor is spread with a Gobelins carpet, one of 93 ordered for the Louvre by Louis XIV in 1664.

The Green Room next to the salon contains a Jacob bed crowned with ostrich plumes and a Riesener desk. This is followed by a sequence of smaller rooms, each carefully restored with period *boiseries*, and a vestibule hung with fleurs-de-lys. However, when the last candles are blown out after yet another party, Garcia retires discreetly to an austere bedroom for a sound night's rest.

ABOVE LEFT   *The paint is still drying on a restored merry-go-round horse.*
ABOVE RIGHT   *The studio area of the main room.*
RIGHT   *Claude Ben Signor lives at the top of this building, overlooking the Seine and the railway lines of the Gare d'Austerlitz.*

"*Give me two or three old pieces of wood and I can settle down nicely.*"
CLAUDE BEN SIGNOR

Claude Ben Signor is a carpenter and sculptor who makes wooden toys and puppets with the aid of his psychoanalyst companion. His children, who live elsewhere, often come to spend the weekend. Ben Signor is a bearded, moustachioed, long-haired man who wears thick brown corduroys and hand-knitted socks; he readily admits that he is a neo-hippie and refugee from 1968 who has come back to the city. His home is on the top floor of an amazing industrial building and consists of three small attic rooms overlooking the Gare d'Austerlitz and the warehouses of Bercy. This no-man's-land, under constant threat of demolition, shelters a profusion of recording studios

ABOVE LEFT   *The kitchen, where the sculptor prepares his various cereal and vegetable dishes.*
ABOVE RIGHT   *Facing the bed is a desk and sculpture by Ben Signor, and a wood-burning stove, which heats the house.*
RIGHT   *The bed in the main room.*

and decorators' workshops; hence the constant blare of music and the mysterious comings and goings at all hours of the day and night. Claude Ben Signor remains unruffled. When he is not working on his sculpture, he studies Hebrew. He loves the Bible, Victor Segalen and Georges Perec, rolls his own cigarettes, eats plenty of cereals and vegetables from a bowl "whenever and wherever he feels the need," and is delighted that his building has been spared by major construction projects. "I could never live in what they call an ordinary apartment," he claims. "I like living in the place where I work. My objects are based

on country habits: first I sculpt them, then I put them to sleep. For me the essential comfort consists in setting up my workbench in a place where there is space, light and sufficient warmth. It was reassuring to discover that I could find just as much wood in garbage cans here in Paris as in the forest I left behind in the country. For example, you come across an ugly old beam lying around somewhere, you open it up and you find brand new oakwood. This place is small, but it's all I need to work. I insist on doing everything myself, on salvaging materials from the street. The more I can do without the help of other people, the happier I am."

"A home without animals is inconceivable."
NATHALIE BARDON

Nathalie Bardon lives in a timeless, tiny Montmartre street. Her husband, Renaud, is one of the architects responsible for conceiving the design of the new Musée d'Orsay.

Dogs, cats, sparrows, canaries, goldfish and guinea pigs share the premises. "I used to be a decorator, but I no longer find it interesting. We have two daughters, Adélaïde and Judith. I've realized now that I only live in town out of necessity and, whenever I get the chance, I go to the country. That's where I'm at my best." Nathalie spends all her weekends and most of the summer at her farm. "Moving down to the country with all my pets and the children is quite an adventure. I've even bought a car specially to transport all the mobile objects. Renaud is in charge of boxes." The Paris house is tall and narrow, with old-fashioned upstairs rooms and long corridors hung with pictures of dogs, cats, donkeys, babies and old women. Downstairs, the garden forces its way through the windows into the house a little more every year. The wisteria and camelias crawl or stretch in, and the rose bushes spread out all over the place. "It's difficult to keep any space for the girls' volleyball games and my tulips and *cœurs de Marie* at the same time. I'm trying to teach my children to respect the garden. Later they'll understand better how important it is for the equilibrium to have a bit of garden."

It's a perpetual battle. The orchids and lemon trees, which flower in summer, are lucky

LEFT   *The living room gives onto the garden. Zephir, Nathalie's elderly dog, occupies the best armchair.*
ABOVE   *The house as it looks from the greenhouse.*
BELOW   *The greenhouse, where Nathalie grows her orchids.*
OVERLEAF   *The corner of the garden assigned to Nathalie's daughters is closed off by a small gate.*

enough to have a corner of a greenhouse that was recovered from a family garden. They have to share this privilege, however, with the guinea pigs and an occasional visiting butterfly. That is, when Nathalie decides to let the cocoons hatch. "Then, I have to find food for them too."

In the house, where the floors are paved with large flagstones from the Midi in which various dogs have left their pawprints, Nathalie has used odd pieces of material to protect the chintz-covered furniture from the dogs and cats that settle down wherever they wish.

After every trip to the country, Nathalie brings something back to add to her collection of wildflowers, nests, rocks and feathers. "I'm always cleaning up, but I must admit that I do like a little mess." On the walls there are prints and paintings depicting scenes from nature: landscapes, farmhouses, delicate rock formations, insects, butterflies, birds, dragonflies and mushrooms. A large farmhouse table, which is surrounded by beautiful Empire- and Directoire-style pieces of family furniture, provides balance in the main room. This room connects to the kitchen, which is too small to eat in. This is no problem in summer because everyone eats in the garden. There is a small study nearby, which is full of books and nature sketches, and allows the adults to escape the joyful noise of children elsewhere in the house. Nathalie has managed to make the whole effect charming — even if the sofas have been chewed by dogs and the lovely raw silk curtains and the carpets have been scratched by cats sharpening their claws. This atmosphere of intimacy and imperfection, in which children, pets and flowers are more important than paintings, chairs or lamps, is reminiscent of one of Vuillard's paintings, especially when a ray of light shines on the corner of a cage or shimmers on the softness of a faded cretonne.

ABOVE   *The bedroom occupied by Nathalie and Renaud has an 18th-century iron bedstead and above it a painted canvas screen from the same period.*
RIGHT   *Cage containing Japanese sparrows.*
BELOW   *General view of the living room, which connects with the kitchen.*

At the back of a courtyard in the Bastille quarter, the painter Gosta Claesson has made his home in an old weighing-machine factory. From the courtyard covered in glass and metal, Claesson has created a space in which he can live and work. The huge area is white, with a tiled entrance, and is lit by neon tubes: it connects with the factory's former office area, which is more or less without natural light. Here Claesson has organized a living area. Claesson is blonde, blue-eyed and almost pathologically obsessed with precision — the archetypal Swede. Three teams of workers tried and failed to carry out his plans for the building: finally, Claesson did it himself. The result is nothing short of perfection, like the *gigot en jambon aux herbes* that he prepares for his friends. Claesson may be described as international. At 20, he worked

RIGHT   *The living room, which is also used as a studio by Claesson, was formerly a factory workshop. The door on the left leads to the kitchen and dining room.*
LEFT   *Detail of the end wall in the living room showing a Flemish painting, figurines and other objects from Africa and New Guinea, and Yemeni jewelry.*
BELOW   *Several yards of pastel colours stretch along the living-room wall.*
OVERLEAF   *The kitchen units are made of oak taken from the former factory offices.*

"*You can't give life to a loft unless you work in it. The space is too huge.*"
GOSTA CLAESSON

58

ABOVE *Another view of the living room, showing a Picasso drawing and an 18th-century German desk.*
RIGHT *The bedroom-alcove is decorated with African fabrics and white tiling.*
BELOW *The bathroom.*

his way around the world on a ship. Subsequently he lived in New York. Claesson has always been partial to difficult enterprises and adventures: once he lived alone in the Yemen for two years.

Today, he is haunted by images of Africa, and the violent colours of statues and masks he brought back enliven his white loft. Africa and Europe co-exist peacefully here: the 1930 red lacquer French armoire, the 18th-century black secretaire from Germany, the Picasso on its easel and the small 17th-century Flemish painting of an executioner represent Europe. To create reflected light, the blind side of the apartment has been covered in white tiling. A sense of warmth and intimacy has been produced by slicing up the old office furniture, stripping it of paint and using it to panel the kitchen and

dining room. In his bedroom Claesson has extended along the walls the indigo motifs of African textiles, which are reflected by his Louis XIII mirror, made of polished red horn.

The only light in the apartment comes from the sky, so Claesson is effectively cut off. This, he maintains, is good for his concentration on painting and his peace of mind, all the more so because he maintains an iron discipline. As a perfectionist, Claesson always paints for five to six hours daily, in an attempt to add to his achievements.

ABOVE *Part of the main salon.* RIGHT *The quiet cul-de-sac off the Place Pigalle where the Lafons live.*

"When one's alone in this house, one can feel that people have had a good time here." FRANÇOISE LAFON

Françoise Lafon and her husband André, a businessman, are both unconditional Morocco-lovers. They spend their time commuting between the Palmeraie in Marrakesh and their apartment in Pigalle, where they live at the end of a twisting, tree-lined cul-de-sac, in a backwater away from the night-time crowds and neon lights.

It only took Françoise Lafon a few days to decide on this strange location, as she had sensed its great potential almost immediately. The apartment consists of a series of large and small rooms, spread over several floors. In fact, it can scarcely be called a house except in a special sense: it was formerly "La Maison de Shangai," a celebrated brothel at the turn of the century. Toulouse-Lautrec's studio was just around the corner, amid similar neo-Gothic, Moorish and Greek-style buildings. People came to the old "Maison de Shangai" to play cards, attend plays and above all to meet beautiful "creatures." The house was decorated with red, black and gold chinoiseries in 1900, but these were altered in 1920, when the rose-patterned friezes and columns running along the walls of the main ballroom

were added. This area now serves as a salon and office. Françoise began her conversion work 15 years ago with her friend Jacques Grange, and afterwards continued the work alone, while fixing up houses for other people at the same time.

When Françoise arrived, remnants of ornate décor still survived here and there. Her first instinct was to simplify everything while preserving the essential spirit of the place, which she found to be "full of poetry and illusion."

The basic structure and the various levels of the ballroom were retained, while the tiny office was upholstered in red with a large Oriental sofa in celebration of the old "Shangai" spirit. The turn-of-the-century Orientalist vogue is echoed in Françoise Lafon's bedroom, which has been fitted with Egyptian *boiseries* discovered by Jacques Grange. These *boiseries* came from the theatre of the Comtesse Greffuhle, the model for Proust's Duchesse de Guermantes.

The Egyptian theme reappears in the bathroom's colours, mirrors and stained-glass dating from 1900. Perhaps the most striking feature of the Egyptian suite adjoining the ballroom is its emphasis on refinement as opposed to anecdote. The place is more comfortable than amusing, more subtle than Oriental, with

LEFT *The bathroom echoes some of the Orientalist colours and atmosphere of the bedroom but also contains numerous Arts and Crafts touches.*
RIGHT *The turquoise-and-tan décor of the Egyptian bedroom. In the foreground is a painted Russian chair and choupatte "cabbage with legs" by Claude Lalanne.*

its beiges, turquoises and discreet touches of matt gold. Moreover, Lafon has not hesitated to take decorative liberties both with this extravagant room, and with her bathroom, by sprinkling them with Arts and Crafts and even Russian furniture from the turn of the century. Lafon is a beautiful woman who maintains that many of her dreams concern her house; in her waking hours she tries to make those dreams reality. The level above has a broad, cunningly concealed terrace that connects with the small salon-cum-library, an area that has been handled with a soft intimacy that recalls Bérard or de Lila de Nabili. "I was trying to achieve a sense of lightness, an unfinished quality," Lafon explains. The kitchen is adjacent, charmingly arranged with *boiseries*, and a second bedroom which is unfinished. The bathroom here looks Moorish, though, in fact, it has been entirely constructed around ceramic tiles of the 1880's. The house has a small tower at each end, used by any grandchildren who may be passing through. These tiny areas somehow give the impression that they connect with another house, another terrace, perhaps even an atelier. This is indeed a place of mystery, only accessible to initiates.

"Silence is something we all need, and the ability to achieve it is a great blessing."
JEAN-PIERRE RAYNAUD

The home of sculptor Jean-Pierre Raynaud developed in an inner suburb of Paris amid a host of highly conventional *pavillons* (detached houses).

The nearby railway station is small, as is the street, with its low garden hedges. There is no doorbell and no nameplate. It was begun by its owner some 20 years ago, and initially had no windows. Ever since

Raynaud has been rethinking and altering aspects of it. "I built this place myself," he says, "and it makes no concessions. I take full responsibility for it, I possess it, and I am the one who makes it

RIGHT *View of the house from just inside the gate.* LEFT *Funerary urns and old fabrics in the white interior.* OVERLEAF *The salon.*

66

function. I don't even have a cleaning woman."

Today, Raynaud's house is superbly lit by Renaissance-style windows looking out on blue conifers, and it is now a more serene place in which to live. "People sometimes tell me they could never live here; my response is, I can't see any reason why they should want to live in someone else's womb anyway. This is a private place, shut off from the world." Raynaud's home is neither a house nor a sculpture; it is more a combination of the two. He has opted to inhabit it

during certain phases of his life, a decision similar to that of Montville with his Doric column in the Désert de Retz. Inside, the walls are painted dead white. Raynaud works on a cube of concrete and ceramic tiles facing two broad bay windows, and sleeps in a canopied bed set before a log fire. The bed, which is made with the same tiles as the cube, is covered in 17th-century brocade "which reminds some people of a funeral shroud." Daily functions such as eating and washing are here kept separate. "I have breakfast and

wash myself just like other people," explains Raynaud, "only I don't ritualize these acts. The places of washing and eating have no importance for me." Meals, along with social activities, are conducted "elsewhere. There are no crumbs here. This house is like a hermit's cell; when I'm in it I experience no relational problems. What I have is silence, a resource of immense value that no one who seeks after deeper meanings in the world can afford to do without. To achieve silence, one needs very thick walls, and these are

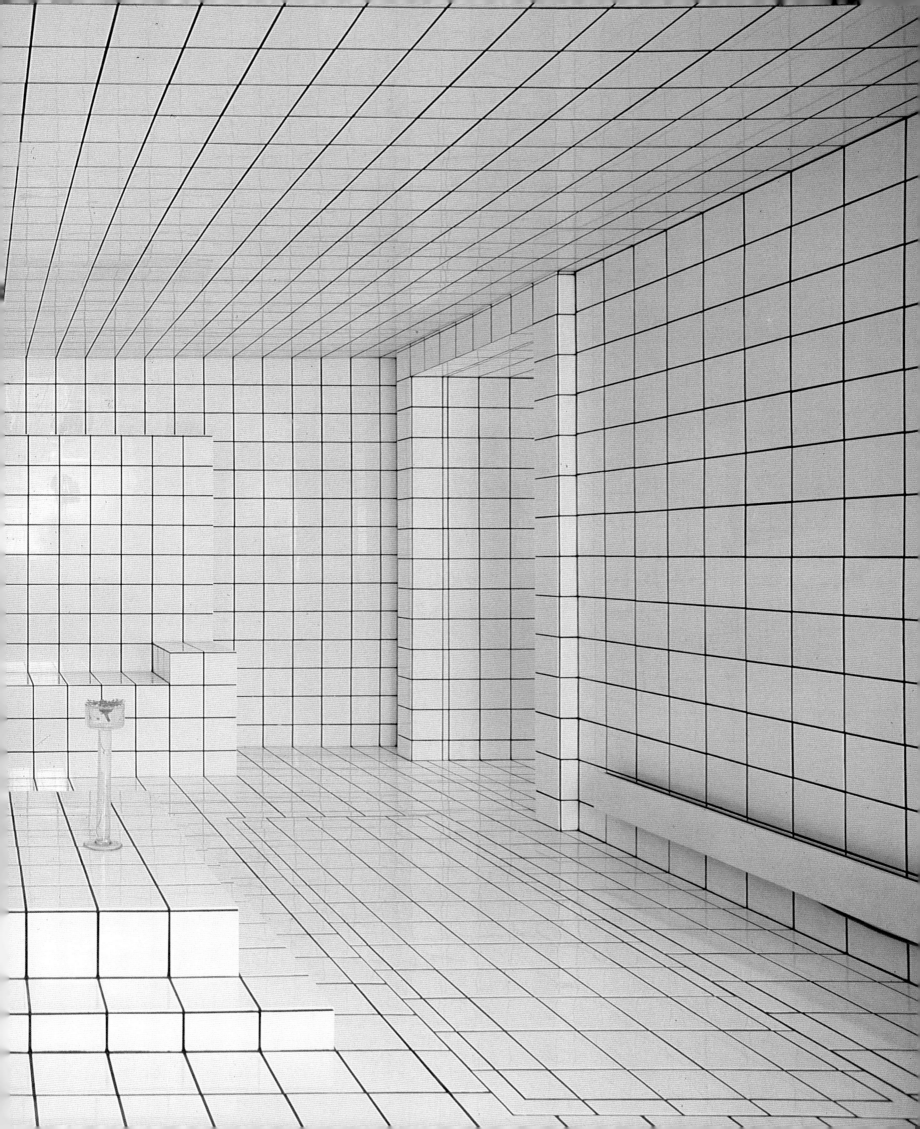

a great luxury. Tiling, which I used from 1964 onwards, abandoned, then took up again in 1972, is a medium linked to this idea of thickness: if it wasn't, there would be no sense in my using it. I resort to white by instinct, I've no idea why. Somehow, I want things to be cold, slippery and intangible."

Despite what Raynaud says, even in midwinter the hard, implacably white interior gives a sensation of great warmth and well-being. The floor, the walls, the ceiling and the tiled furniture — all are made of immovable concrete and ceramic, built into the body of the structure "like Berber mud architecture." On the floor, carpets are represented by breaks in the lines of tiles, creating a new pattern. On the walls, clusters of tiled reliefs serve as substitutes for pictures. The house is divided into two levels, and includes an office, a salon and a bedroom. There are successive corridors and thick window embrasures, which recall the Italian quattrocento, then staircases and more corridors, suggesting the architecture of the Middle Ages and even that of Egypt. Then one comes upon a series of antique objects (always placed on surfaces, never hung on walls), which represent other people and the outside world, and there are always fresh-cut flowers and music. There are even trees rooted in the floor, in places where one or two tiles have been removed to give them space, and flowers in urns. The urn is Raynaud's archetypal form, on which he based his exhibit at the São

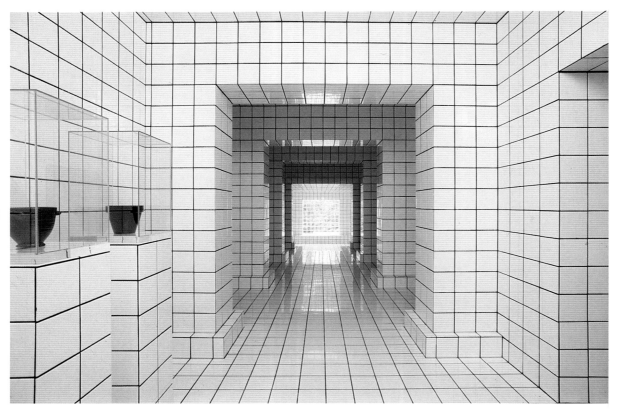

LEFT *Series of corridors leading to the office.*
RIGHT TOP AND CENTRE *Details of the office, which opens onto the garden.*
RIGHT BOTTOM *Detail of the salon.*
PREVIOUS PAGE *In the bedroom quattrocento-style window and 17th-century brocade.*

Paulo Biennale in 1967 when his work was chosen to represent France. Raynaud was, in fact, trained as a landscape gardener, and Pontus Hulten in Stockholm was one of the first critics to praise his sculpture.

Raynaud is determined never again to expose his living space to the public, no matter how select that public may be. In the future, he wants to keep more in the background. "After all this time," he says reflectively, "I don't regret building this house. It regenerates me. I'm not really a mystic, since I'm an atheist, but I believe this is a place of beauty, capable of conveying messages to the human soul. When I cross my threshold and face the world outside, I have a special perspective on it.... I have one attitude when I'm at home, and another when I'm elsewhere, but this doesn't make me vulnerable. On the contrary, it affords me protection."

72

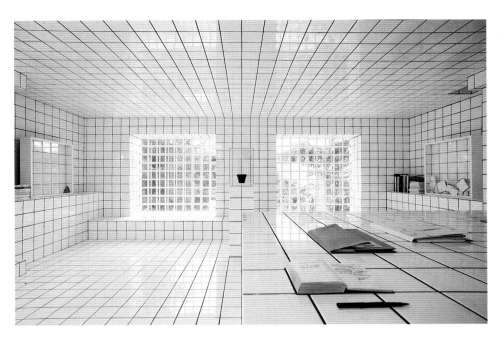

*"I would have wanted to live here
when I was little."*
DAVID ROCHELINE

David Rocheline is half-elf, half-gipsy. He also combines the professions of singer and musical comedy producer; his most recent success is *Gipsy Boy*. Rocheline lives with Pascale Lafay in an unused suburban factory, close to a railway station and a metro. The surrounding area is one of unrelieved concrete, which is not without a certain dark romance at the end of the day.

Rocheline made his décor himself, out of plaster, papier-mâché and cardboard paste. He maintains that nothing in his home cost more than 150FF; even so, it is clear that he is a discerning buyer. His culture is sophisticated, much influenced by 1940's cinema, old comic strips and songs. He is a very funny man, whose humour is at times as desperate as it is side splitting. The house is entered by a monumental staircase. "They're château steps," says Rocheline. "Before, it was completely bare here, except for wooden stairs, which reminded me of school. I

ABOVE   *The salon with its false marble tiles, false drapes and false Genoa velvet painted on the sofa.*
RIGHT   *The Gothic staircase leading to David's office.*

decided to hide all that with a Venetian balustrade made of 10mm plywood." Next comes an enormous hallway, leading up to a Renaissance-style gallery, with the salon and bedrooms adjacent.

Overlooking the staircase is a curving theatre balcony. "It's the same one Cocteau used in *La Belle et la Bête*," explains Rocheline. Behind this balcony (which one is forbidden to lean against) is a bathroom resembling a theatre box. Pascale and David disagree; for them it's merely Spanish, on the lines of Pierre Louÿs's *The Women and the Puppet*. In the salon, which quivers periodically to the rhythm of trains, are huge sofas covered in yellow damask; Rocheline is ashamed of these, and is painting them over with Renaissance petit point. At the end of the room, between two theatre curtains, one can glimpse a distant château at the end of an *allée à la française*.

All the objects in the house, from Baroque to 1950's, were originally bartered for, bought at the Vanves fleamarket or fished out of trash cans. A steep concrete stairway leads from the salon to Rocheline's atelier, as if to a tower. The entrance is by way of a Gothic doorway with ponderous iron fittings made of cardboard, set in a kind of cave-mouth. "I got many of my ideas from the Musée Grévin's French history display," says Rocheline. "I resemble that pauper in the Abel Gance film who paints pictures of the food he dreams of all over the wall. I want my place to look wealthy but trashy, like the rich people in *Les Pieds Nickelés*."

Pascale's small bedroom is in stark contrast to Rocheline's. She collects Barbie dolls, religious statuettes, shells and mirrors and he started out wanting a dark log-cabin, but never got round to painting the logs.

Now, after five years, David Rocheline is beginning to tire of decorating. "For example, I *must* have some Venetian torchères! And I want my bathroom covered in enamelled brickwork like in Granada. I'll arrange a dinner or a birthday party for these projects like I did with the others. You know, to tell you the truth, I don't like *trompe l'œil*; I just happen to be a poor artist. In fact, I long for it all to be real."

ABOVE *The bathroom whose decoration was inspired by the play* The Lady and the Puppet.
RIGHT *The entrance stairway is overlooked by a Spanish-style balcony incorporating the bathroom.*
PREVIOUS PAGE *The stairs leading from the salon, with a cardboard table originally used as a theatre prop. and a pirate's treasure chest.*

Roxane Debuisson's home is on the edge of the Marais, in a turn-of-the-century building with windows of rich stained glass. The apartment is large, the carpeting is beige, and mouldings and golden doorknobs are everywhere. "I'm a real bourgeoise, but I'm also a dedicated Parisian," announces Roxane. She has worked as a volunteer at the Bibliothèque Historique for the last 20 years and is married to a computer-scientist-turned-publisher.

The extravagant objects that bedeck the apartment are the result of two decades of collecting in the streets of Paris. Many of them were discovered, coveted and finally bought over many years.

Debuisson's collection of old Paris postcards is probably the finest in existence, and it was thanks to these that some of her eighty-odd shop signs and craftsmen's insignia were located. They date from between the Second Empire and 1914; most are very large, designed to be hung 10 or 12 feet above the pavement and seen from a distance. They include the carrots, golden snails and red boots beloved of the Prévert brothers and the photographer Robert Doisneau. The writer Claude Mauriac is said to have received a shock when he visited Roxane and discovered a sign that hung on the Avenue Mozart outside a toyshop he had loved as a child, and which had disappeared.

It is "disappearances" like this that Roxane labours to avert. Refacings of buildings, shifts in fashion and changes of

ABOVE RIGHT *The hall contains most of the collection.*
LEFT *Coats are placed on a former park bench, under the blackamoor sign of a* teinturier *(dyer) and the* carotte *sign of a tobacconist.*

" 'What a funny feeling to see 19 years of my life hanging up there on your wall,' the baker's wife told me on entering the dining room."
ROXANE DEBUISSON

ownership are her enemies. Her last resort is to salvage what she can, for she prefers to see the signs where they belong, in the street. Her first piece was acquired out of nostalgia, when she noticed the disappearance of a golden ball with a black ponytail which had decorated the barbershop on her street. She enquired after it and finally purchased it for 50 francs from the barber, who thought it too old-fashioned.

The most recent acquisition is "L'Ours Martin," a sign from a café on the corner of the Rue aux Ours and the Boulevard Saint-Martin. "They've renamed the place 'Djurdjura,'" notes Roxane. The hunt is frequently arduous: one must mark the quarry; one must know in advance whether a demolition has been planned; and finally, one must be willing to pay since removing, dismantling and restoring these objects can be expensive. "It took me nearly 20 years to get this golden glove," she relates. "Every 12 months I went to the glovemaker's. 'Oh, it's you again,' he'd grumble. But I got it in the end."

"I tracked down that golden sun at a dinner party, because I make a point of asking people where they live. In this case I came across someone who lived on the Rue de Turenne. I remembered there'd once been a golden sun there, and asked him if he knew what had become of it. It'd been in his cellar for years." Roxane frequently lends her collection for exhibitions and has bequeathed it to the Musée Carnavalet. She has had disappointments; she has never been able to acquire a golden horse's head. Likewise, her husband draws the line at bringing green Wallace fountains and old-fashioned cast iron *pissoirs* up to the fourth floor, because of the weight. But she consoles herself with her giant snails, spectacles and gloves, her red metro furniture and tree grills. It is also rumoured that this woman, who dines off monogrammed tablecloths, sometimes takes her friends round town on an antiquated platform bus.

ABOVE *In the dining room the table is laid for tea with a pastel-coloured Sarreguemines service and a damask tablecloth. The statue of Leander on the right is an 18th-century shop sign.*
RIGHT *The 1950's kitchen has remained unaltered. The golden snail was the sign of the snail-seller, who operated in much the same way as today's oyster vendors.*

LEFT   *The house at the end of the cul-de-sac, in its Monet-like colours.*
RIGHT   *The dining room is like a ready-made* jardin d'hiver, *with tablecloth and plates by Primerose Bordier and Napoleon III petit point chairs.*

Carole Weisweiller is a television producer. She lives in a "thieves' alley" in the XIVth *arrondissement* and behind the tall iron gate bearing her initials is the most romantic little house in Paris. Like Monet's *pavillon* at Giverny, it is all pinks and greens. Carole rejoices in the shade of her magnificent fig tree. "I don't have curtains in the salon because I want to let the garden in." On the first floor, where the rooms are filled with light, she has compromised with curtains of green silk, lush as a lime tree. The house is suffused with gaiety, dominated by the subtle play of pink and green. A green verandah leads off the pink main body of the house,

"*What's vital is knowing how to create a place in one's own image.*"
CAROLE WEISWEILLER

life, Madeleine Castaing and Jean Cocteau.

Castaing's first commission as a decorator had been a house north of Paris belonging to Weisweiller's mother in 1947. "I admire Madeleine, and I'm also fond of her. Her husband, Marcellin, was a delicious creature, Proustian to a fault." All Carole's 19th-century furniture comes from Rue Jacob, but the atmosphere of her house is joyous and sunlit, rather than sombre and nostalgic like the Castaing original. As for Cocteau, whose signed drawings and photographs are present everywhere, Carole refers to him as "my spiritual father. He lived at my mother's house throughout my childhood and adolescence." The false piano in the salon, which turns out to be a gramophone, is perhaps the most interesting object in the house. A profusion of books about theatre, cinema, music and stage and film direction complete the portrait of Carole Weisweiller.

and connects with a kitchen of the same shade. There are plants everywhere, offset by ubiquitous bamboo and turquoise-and-tan tiling of the 1900's. The effect in the dining room is of a pool of light centred on the dining table and the black Second Empire chairs.

The remainder of the ground floor is divided in two by the "entrance hall," which does not exist as a definite entity, as all the adjacent areas are wide open. Two sides, for example, are part of a salon and a library.

"Naturally, everyone likes harmony and beauty in a house, but are they really crucial? I think the main thing is to create an atmosphere of gaiety. The skilful juxtaposition of colours can be as important as valuable furniture. If I lived in a classified building, I would perhaps think otherwise. As it is I'm lucky to have a house: to me it's a complete entity, a complete country and a complete universe. But there's no denying it's a bit kitsch, a bit Rococo even — the house used to belong to a sculptor, so

I wouldn't dream of giving it 18th-century airs. You can't change the character of a house any more than you can that of a man."

Whatever Carole says, her presence has been decisive. When she arrived, the house was painted grey and the garden was derelict: her first move was to restore the architecture, with the assistance of de Graaf and Jouve. With the building stripped to essentials and the garden remodelled around its fig tree, Carole brought to bear the two major influences of her

Emmanuel Pereire occupies the top floor of a tall, modern building in the Bercy quarter of Paris. There is a 360-degree view of the city, including the Eiffel Tower, Sacré-Cœur and the new Opéra de la Bastille. When night falls, the apartment seems suspended between two starry skies: this is not surprising when one considers that Pereire likes to describe himself as an *"angélologue,"* a specialist in the study of angels. His first exhibition was held at the Knoedler Gallery in New York in 1965; the catalogue preface was by Barthes, who admired Pereire's versatility; he had arrived at painting by way of writing, photography, theatre and experimental physics. Nonetheless, Pereire is relatively unknown in France; his success has been mostly in the United States, where he has mounted important exhibitions at the Museum of Modern Art in New York. He is interested in the angel as a symbol of communication, and his talk is full of references to light, space, emptiness, flying and falling. Looking through the windows, one cannot avoid being struck by the parallels between his high abode and

RIGHT   *On the 20th floor: the studio and the terrace.*
BELOW   *The 180-degree view of Paris at dusk.*

"I live in a bunker overlooking the world."
EMMANUEL PEREIRE

ABOVE AND BELOW *Views of the salon, with a table sculpture by Jean-Louis Faure.* RIGHT *One of Pereire's little art "installations" in front of a painting completed in March 1988.*
OVERLEAF *A bedroom-cum-library, where the window is masked by one of Pereire's compositions,* Triomphe de la Mort de la Peinture.

the figures in his paintings. "I've always dreamed of having nobody overhead." he remarks. "But one must go through a miniature hell before one can reach heaven, and that's exactly as it should be." It's true that the approach to Pereire's penthouse is somewhat disheartening. There is a lift and dark, windowless landings. Finally one is admitted into a bright salon, separated from the outer void by a screen of laurel. "You should try to think of the sky, not of falling," says Pereire reassuringly. The floor is covered with a corded carpet; the contents of the room are two 1930's indigo-blue chairs (ripped to shreds by the cats),

an old mat from Indonesia and a Knoll couch worn threadbare by the clients of Pereire's psychoanalyst girlfriend. Clearly, the man who lives here is somebody who attaches importance to signs. "The space that produces an object is more important than the object itself," notes Pereire; thus friendship is signified by a table made by Jean-Louis Faure or one given by Andrée Putman, and humour by the couch, which seems drenched in the fantasies of the analysands who have lain on it. Another of Pereire's obsessions is the message from a forgotten civilization. In each of the small interchangeable cells (semi-bedroom, semi-library,

semi-salon) which make up his apartment, there is a messenger object. On the Biedermeyer commode is a bird's egg, 54 million years old, and over the television is draped a necklace of human bones fashioned into death's heads. "For an object to be a treasure in my eyes, it must offer a leap in time like a leap into the void," says Pereire. "Whether the piece is an Egyptian vase from the New Empire, or some ancient shard of stone, it can give me the impression of possessing a fragment of eternity." All the same, the situation and surroundings of this apartment are considerably stronger than the objects it contains. Every room (and there are two floor levels) opens directly onto a terrace or a sheer drop. The outside is inevitably masked by bookshelves, a picture or blinds; Pereire must be aware that the association of the adjacent chasm with his canvases of fallen angels is disquieting.

In general, Pereire's decoration is restricted by the cheap architecture of the space he lives in; hence his décor is sober to the point of nullity. There are no curtains and no wall fabrics, for example. What this artist manifestly desires is a sense of precariousness, insecurity, vertigo: witness the single coat of transparent blue paint on the walls of the bedroom, which can only be reached by crossing an open terrace in the teeth of the wind. In this modest room, which has the charm of certain cheap hotels in Africa or Greece, the images of Gabriel, Icarus and Lucifer are not so far away. Meanwhile, the cats lounge about luxuriously, and sunset burnishes La Défense.

ABOVE   *Detail of a painting in the yellow salon.*
LEFT   *The courtyard, quintessentially Parisian, shows traces of several different periods.*
BELOW   *The ground-floor entrance.*

"I like accumulations of things on my walls; I see them as a bastion against death."
BERNARD MINORET

Bernard Minoret is a playwright with a passion for history, living in a quiet street of the Faubourg Saint-Germain, that incomparable pocket of French civilization. A friend and neighbour, the writer Geneviève Dormann, describes him as follows: "The Minoret we know and love moves about with infinite caution. In the last 20 years, he has not ventured beyond the Rue de Lille and the Rue de Verneuil... it's good to have a Minoret in the vicinity, particularly if one needs a dictionary... at any time of day or night, he will supply information about the colour of Aimée de Coigny's ribbon, what the Prince de Ligne was doing on September 24, 1783, or the erotic tastes of Claude Gellée, known as Le Lorrain. But most of all, a Minoret is essential in the event of personal difficulty. Broken hearts, and other such complaints which are our daily lot in this valley of tears, stand no chance against his ferociously myopic wit...." Bernard Minoret's two-floor apartment is like nothing so much as an old village house somewhere in the Sarthe department of France ... or even the Somme. The entrance is gloomy to a degree, with an 18th-century monumental oak door and a creaking staircase. A heap of loden coats, umbrellas, scarves and pigskin gloves await their master on the Louis-Philippe hall chairs. Already, one can perceive the keynote for the entire apartment in the red-and-gold wall fabric: "I like walls to be covered in fabric," says Bernard Minoret. "I think it gives one extra protection; and fabrics are less movable than pictures, which can be shifted about at whim." On the first floor, a long L-shaped corridor leads to the yellow salon, the bedroom and the kitchen, which last is more or less what one might expect of an intellectual who always eats away from home. Nonetheless, there are two gas rings for making tea, which Minoret dispenses in the afternoons to friends who come to talk theatre. In general, the house is highly convivial, an excellent place to spend a Sunday afternoon in company with the host's 18th-century terracotta

busts of Rachel, Marat, Pauline Borghese and others. The late 18th century is Bernard Minoret's favourite period in history: "I think these people's faces end up belonging to me," he notes. "I also think it is possible to establish a kind of complicity between the conversation one is having and the audience of pictures on the wall. When I juxtapose Revolutionary and Ancien Régime objects, I do so because I feel kinship with both. I see myself as an innovator and victim in the realm of intelligence; like Marie-Antoinette, but also like Robespierre."
The slightly formal salon blends family furniture and portraits with more recent acquisitions; in the main, it resembles an old-fashioned French living room. Bernard Minoret rejects this idea. "I hate that word. This is a place for talking; what I like is a room that combines the virtues of intimacy and dignity. The colours are inspired by Balzac. I'm rather gratified when people find it elegant."
In the adjoining bedroom objects yield their pride of place to books, which threaten to engulf the small antique bed. "Since the enemy habitually approaches from the rear, one

The yellow salon. The divan on the left, which is casually draped with a kashmir shawl, and a table by Diego Giacometti face family portraits and scenes painted by Pernet and Hubert Robert, as well as terracotta busts of revolutionary figures — the owner's "friends."

98

should always sleep in a corner among one's books," is Minoret's comment. The decorator Hubert de la Marinière has attempted to organize and contain this avalanche of literature with shrewdly-conceived shelves. Near the bed are a pile of newspapers, the latest book on Chamfort (written by a friend), a bottle of Evian water and a television, as well as two or three busts and engravings — reminders of Minoret's attachments to Cocteau, Dora Maar, Picasso, Marie-Laure de Noailles and Leonor Fini. Fini painted Minoret's portrait when the latter was 25. The bathroom is not unlike an actor's dressing room in a theatre, with the drapery on the tub, the antiquated niche,

the profusion of marble and the weird light. Here also an invasion is under way; this time the interlopers are not books but boxes, vials and bottles of uncertain age, origin and content.

All in all, Bernard Minoret's apartment takes no account of appearances and conforms to no rule. It is the home of an amusing, cultivated bohemian in the English mould. "I like nightlife, theatres and bistros," Minoret confesses. "My way is the absolute opposite of efficient American-style living. I detest diligent people. Discipline is fair enough, but only if it is totally invisible."

RIGHT *The bedroom-cum-library, with a Russian chair in the foreground.*
BELOW *The Parisian intellectual's kitchen.*

100

Barbara Wirth, the decorator, lives with her engineer husband on Place du Palais Bourbon, in a first-floor apartment overlooking a courtyard. At the entrance, she has installed laurel and box topiary, overlooked by white geraniums. To some extent, these flowers relieve their owner's nostalgia for gardens, a nostalgia which elsewhere in her home generates bouquets of old roses, stephanotis growing in pots, thyme and moss on tables and the traditional December bulbs in blue vases; the bulbs, we are told, have just replaced the scented English geraniums, rare orchids and tropical plants that thrive on air alone. Wirth is not only a passionate botanist, but a great lover of and student of colour, and it is this which lends sparkle to a home that, though part of a beautiful building, might otherwise appear conventional.

The apartment is laid out in classical fashion, with 18th-century proportions. There are two large rooms at the front, with a salon and bedroom forming an angle with a library. The dining room, kitchen and children's bedrooms look over the courtyard and function as a second apartment with a separate entrance. The majestic main entrance has a high ceiling and the floor is tiled in black and white; an 18th-century grey leather settee invites the visitor to take off his coat and leave it there. On all four sides of the hall are *trompe l'œil* cypress trees painted by Timothy Hennessy, each with its own little watering can: a foretaste of the owner's love of plants and gaiety. The family dog, a golden retriever, completes the impression that one has

BELOW AND RIGHT *The apartment overlooks the Palais Bourbon and backs onto a small courtyard full of geraniums.* LEFT *In the entrance, Timothy Hennessy's yew trees frame an 18th-century chair.*

"I don't insist that everything is sumptuously beautiful. All I want for a house is that it is tasteful."
BARBARA WIRTH

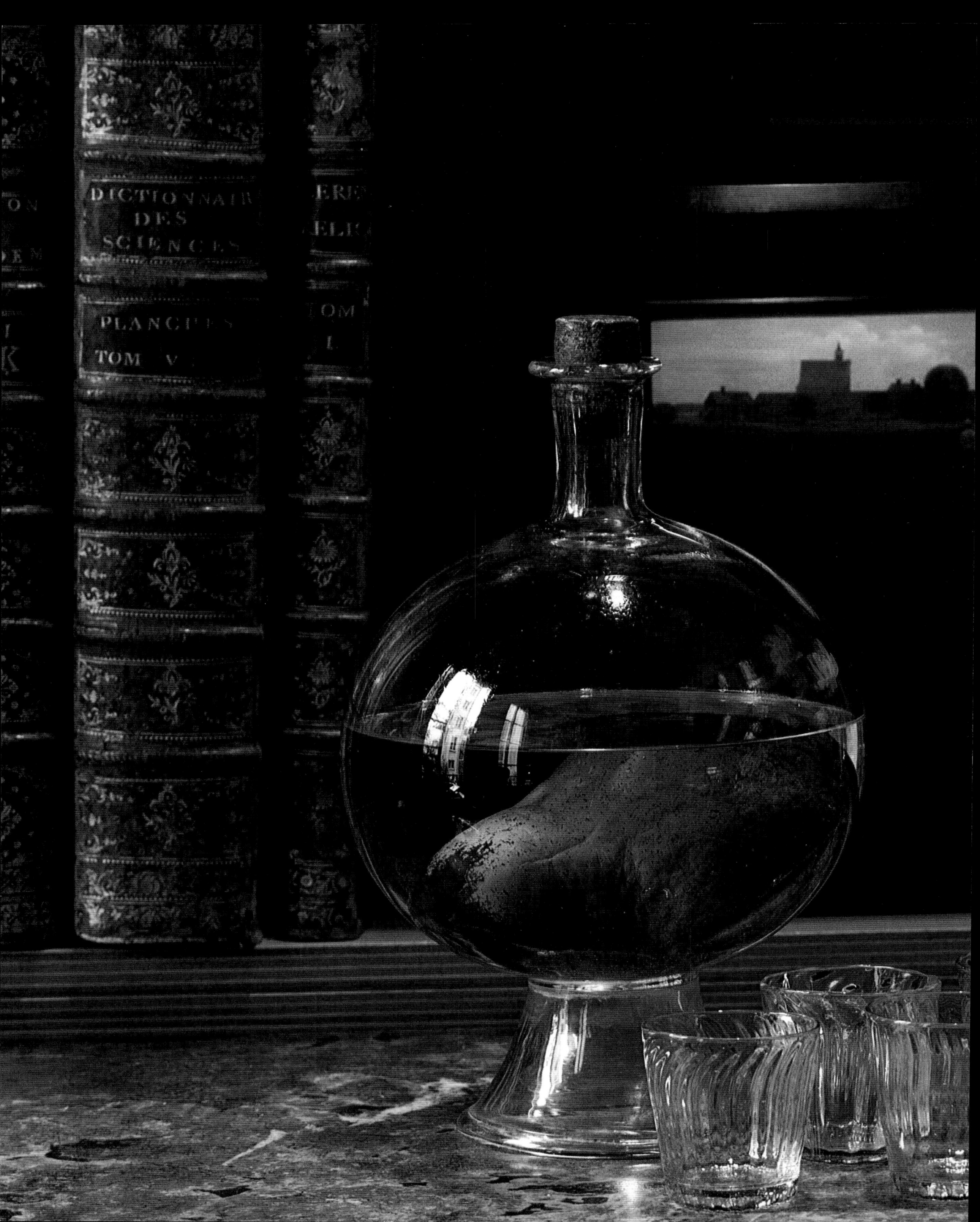
DES
SCIENCES
TOM V

LEFT *The dining room in summer, with green wall tiles, flower-painted chairs by Christian Badin and a batik tablecloth.*
RIGHT *The bedroom, with its unbleached cotton draperies, overlooks the Palais Bourbon*
BELOW RIGHT *In the white salon a mask by Courtright stands on a Giacometti table in company with various small animals. The chairs are by Christian Badin.*
PAGES *104-5 The green-and-pink library, with its strong English influence contains an 18th-century cavalier's chair, Chesterfield sofa and Giacometti armchair.*
PREVIOUS PAGE *Detail of the library with a painting by Philippe Saalburg behind a bottle of Eau de Vie de Poire.*

wandered into an elegant country house.

From here one proceeds to the drawing room by way of the library; indeed, the two are difficult to dissociate. The colours in the library are muted — this is a place for intimate conversation, where Laphroaig whisky is drunk and smoke of Havana cigars clouds the air. Ensconced in a purple Louis XIV invalid's chair, one can leaf through Diderot's *Encyclopaedia* or a book on Tuscan gardens. This is a thoroughly civilized room, very English, planned by decorator Christian Badin around the books, which had to be shelved without breaking the rhythm of the mouldings and panels — hence the two series of bookcases, one with and one without a cornice.

Barbara Wirth is an expert at marrying shades of green and pink, and these lively colours admirably set off the white of the salon, which contains *boiseries* repainted by José Maria Sert before the last war. Contemporary canvases, a table by Giacometti and pastel-coloured modern textiles and rugs woven to measure make the room summery. Here, empty space, light and sobriety complement the exuberance of the library; but the latter is echoed by the bedroom, which is shaded by grey-brown linen blinds. The bed itself has a theatrical canopy topped by a pineapple, while the floor is covered by pink wall-to-wall carpeting and a flower-printed rug.

A series of corridors, walled with mirrors, leads past the hidden dressing room and bathroom to a long dining room. Here again, the themes of colour and plant life are dominant. There are several tables, with seating for up to 20 guests: parties are frequent in the Wirth household, which positively radiates festivity and friendliness. On these occasions, Wirth — who is famous for her knack of setting tables — will lay her Chelsea porcelain plates on multicoloured batik tablecloths, while the glasses will be blue like anemones. As she says, "Colour always comes first."

The salon is centred on a round table; on certain memorable occasions, such as her husband's return from wartime prison or their 25th wedding anniversary, 19 people have been counted around this table. The chairs are all matching, while the buffet and the piece that houses the crystal are adorned with 1920's rose garlands. "We bought all these things from an upholsterer friend, who had had them made to his own design. Poor man, he had to retire to the country: he caught tuberculosis while repairing the stage curtain at the Opéra." Touches of bright colour are supplied by artificial flowers; a crystal vase of red plastic roses stands at the centre of Lucie's oil-cloth tablecover. "What with the heat I need at my age, real flowers don't last long enough," she says briskly. "I always say that when people bring me bouquets it's just throwing money away."
In the bedroom, the bed, the mirrored wardrobe and the night table are all made of pine. "They belonged to my husband's brother when he was a boy. That's how old they are!" On the mantelpiece stands a photograph of Lucie's husband, with a sprig of lily-of-the-valley beside it to commemorate his death on 1 May; the same picture, enlarged, hangs above the bed. This is a house in which memories are cherished. After the death of her dog, Chouki (a cross between a cocker spaniel and a pomeranian), Lucie had a portrait of her pet painted from photographs by a neighbour from the print shop.

"What I have here is something I love. I can't see myself in any other place." LUCIE TREIBER

Lucie Treiber is 81 years old. Since 1928 she has lived in Belleville, in a modest building that can only be reached by walking through others that sit in front of it. The building dates from the 19th century and each apartment is allotted a piece of ground. Formerly, these were used as vegetable gardens; today, they are mostly planted with flowers or are left vacant. Lucie Treiber worked from the age of 13 to 65 at a print shop, where her husband (now dead) was a typesetter and her sister-in-law a forewoman. At that time, there were many printers in the neighbourhood. Lucie planted potatoes in her allotment, along with parsley, chervil and tarragon (hard to protect against wandering tomcats). Her father-in-law, who lived in the same building, preferred to raise chickens and tomatoes. During World War II, when her husband was a prisoner for six years, Lucie grew tobacco and sent him the dried leaves. She remembers that during that time a warm summer evening would bring all the tenants out into the garden, where they would water their plants and hoe the weeds. "We were a big family then," recalls Lucie.
Madame Treiber's apartment consists of two connecting rooms and a meticulously clean kitchen. The furnishings were installed during the 1930s, and she has never been tempted to modernize her dwelling. Neat, with a sparkling memory and vivid blue eyes, this lady knows exactly what she wants.

ABOVE *The paved pathway separating the allotments.*
RIGHT *Lucie's dining room, which connects with the bedroom.*

"I loved that dog as if it were my child," she declares. "When he got sick, he used to look at me with enormous intensity, as if to say 'Don't you understand?'"

Lucie is especially proud of the bronze cupids, animals and ashtrays scattered around her house, all of which were cast by her great-uncle. This ancestor was the creator of "Marianne," the female representation of the French Republic that appears on French coins. Other treasured possessions include the green ceramicware that was a present for her silver wedding anniversary and some fine Chinese vases that she recovered when her sister-in-law died.

Everyday Lucie Treiber goes out to do her shopping. She misses the old times, when bands played in the street bandstands, but television is something of a solace. When she's in good spirits, she cooks some excellent dishes. Lucie's life is in perfect harmony with the place in which she lives, and no power on earth could make her change it.

ABOVE LEFT   *The sideboard, with the collection of green 1950's ceramics.*
ABOVE RIGHT   *Lucie's bedroom is dominated by a photograph of her husband.*
RIGHT   *Another photograph of her husband stands on the mantelpiece, surrounded by Chinese vases.*

*"Above all,
a house should make
one feel at ease
— and the Hôtel Lambert
is no exception."*
*MARIE-HÉLÈNE
DE ROTHSCHILD*

ABOVE *The grotto-like recess on the main staircase leads to an inner
courtyard and then to the Hercules Gallery.* RIGHT *The tip of the Ile-Saint-
Louis with the Hôtel Lambert, as seen from the Henri IV bridge.*

On certain evenings, thousands of candles are lit in the windows of the Hôtel Lambert and glimmer through the chestnut trees at the tip of the Ile Saint-Louis. On this particular night, Baron and Baroness Guy de Rothschild are receiving the Queen of Denmark, and whole truckloads of daisies *(marguerites)* have been brought to the Rue Saint-Louis-en-l'Ile to decorate the table in her honour. The green 361-piece Sèvres service — the only one of its kind in the world — has been taken down from the wall it decorates. Thirty servants in long white aprons line up the red damask chairs, and light the candelabras one by one above the forest of Louis XIV crystal glasses. Beneath Lebrun's magnificent painted ceiling, the preparations are lavish without

the least hint of swank. This is a décor worthy of Perrault, and such as we shall rarely, if ever, see again. Meanwhile, in the Hercules Gallery, the atmosphere is almost feverish. The Queen is known to be punctual to a fault.

The Hôtel Lambert has witnessed a Fairy Ball, a Proust Ball, a Surrealist Ball, even an Oriental Ball. "A house for a philosopher-king." was Voltaire's admiring verdict. "Its site is worthy of Constantinople."

The history of the Hôtel Lambert is long and complex. In 1642, J. B. Lambert de Thorigny, a financier, commissioned Louis Le Vau to build him a mansion. Scarcely had the principal work been completed when Le Vau's client died, and it was left to his brother, Nicolas Lambert, also a financier, to complete the interior décor with the help

of Charles Le Brun and Eustache Le Sueur. The trio of Le Brun, Le Sueur and Le Vau was later immortalized as "Les Trois Le."

The home remained in the Lambert family until the mid-18th century, when it passed to a series of Farmer Generals of Taxes, before its acquisition by the Marquise de Châtelet, Voltaire's mistress.

By the beginning of the 19th century, it had fallen into poor repair and was purchased by Adam Czartovitsky, a Polish prince. Czartovitsky's heirs sold the building to the Rothschilds in 1975.

The layout of the Hôtel Lambert is complicated. The monumental gateway on the Rue Saint-Louis-en-l'Ile leads onto a square courtyard surrounded by two-storeyed buildings. Towards the tip of the island, a right-angled wing extends from the central body,

ABOVE *The bedroom of Marie-Hélène de Rothschild has Boulle furniture, 17th-century Genoa velvet wall fabric and paintings by Sebastiano del Piombo, Van Scorel and Quentin Metsys.*
RIGHT *Detail of the bedroom showing four 17th-century Florentine busts of Caesar in front of a screen decorated with Limoges enamelling.*
PREVIOUS PAGE *Two small Renaissance cabinets de curiosité, or collection rooms, on the first floor, one containing Limoges enamelware, the other an assortment of Italian majolicas.*

creating a space for the garden. The second floor of this wing contains the celebrated Hercules Gallery, with its ceiling by Le Sueur and décor by Van Hobstal. On either side of this second floor are various formal salons, among them the marvellous Salon des Muses decorated by Le Brun. Below, on the first floor, Marie-Hélène de Rothschild has taken the risk of transforming a historical space into a liveable home, drawing on the inimitable Rothschild knack for blending comfort with

magnificence. To breathe new life into the abandoned rooms, she chose Renzo Mongiardino, Zeffirelli's decorator. "He has both the culture and the *savoir-faire*," she explains enthusiastically. "We worked on the project hand-in-glove." He was instructed to install a whole array of treasures by such masters as Riesener, Jacob, Boulle, Greuze, Gainsborough, Bernard Palissy and others, and to place each work in such a way that the effect would be neither museum, nor château, but home. Perhaps the most astonishing rooms in the Hôtel Lambert are the smaller ones, which are decorated in the manner of *cabinets de curiosité* (collection rooms). The first is full of 16th-century Limousin enamelware, mainly portraits, and the second is devoted to 16th-century Spanish and Italian faïence. One scarcely has time to recover from this before one is stupefied anew by the bedroom, with its gold-embroidered Genoa velvet walls, and a small salon upholstered with Cordoba leather.

Alongside all this magnificence, one is charmed by the unobtrusive presence of such familiar things as flowers, family photographs and small, obviously intimate objects. Here and there one comes across an enamel butterfly, a tiny piece of mother-of-pearl or an ivory rosary; in short, things that bear witness to old infatuations and friendships and wait patiently under lampshades for their turn to be talked about.

Marie-Hélène de Rothschild plays the Hôtel Lambert like some magical musical instrument that can produce a thousand different sounds to enchant her friends. The site is incomparable, the collections are extraordinary and the hostess is a flamboyant personality with a passionate respect for her home.

122

ABOVE   *The cabinet de porcelaine where the green Sèvres service is normally kept along with an extraordinary "commode" that formerly belonged to Mademoiselle de Sens.*
RIGHT   *The Hercules Gallery, where, surrounded by the décor of Van Obstal and Le Brun, the table has been laid with the Sèvres service for the Queen of Denmark.*
PREVIOUS PAGE   *The pink boudoir, below the Hercules Gallery, looks onto the garden and the Seine. This room was "Orientalized" by Mongiardino and Doboujinski.*

I wanted a *pompier* (ornate) apartment," explains Yves Gastou; "what I didn't want was a loft full of dead-looking things." Gastou is a collector and dealer in contemporary art; he lives with his wife, Françoise, his son, Victor, and Nana, the family dog, in a apartment just around the corner from the Madeleine. Their style of life is classic, except that almost every object they possess is the creation of a contemporary artist. Among these are Ettore Sottsass, whom Gastou calls

RIGHT *The Napoleon III salon, with the Gastou's contemporary "post-Memphis" pieces: 1950's table by Carlo Molino, paintings by J. M. Meister and chairs by Mendini and Kuramata.*
BELOW *View of the office with 19th-century stained-glass and a 1922 bronze by H. Ward.*

"I matched an overblown Secon

Empire style with objects from our own time." YVES GASTOU

"The Master," Gaetano Pesce, Kuramata, Carlo Molino and Dubreuil. Yet Gastou is worried by people's reactions. "I can't understand why they find our apartment so astonishing."

By the age of 15, Gastou, in his native Carcassonne, was already collecting everything he could lay his hands on. At 17, he started to react against current tastes; the first Gallé vase he saw altered his life completely. Before long he had opened an Art Deco and Art Nouveau shop in Toulouse; he also had a stand at the fleamarket, where he met Françoise, a law student. The couple began buying objects from the 1950's and decided to move to Paris. They arrived with high expectations in 1985, to open a shop in Rue Bonaparte. The outcry over its futurist design was so intense that Minister of Culture, Jack Lang, had to intervene. The décor was arranged by the Italian post-Modernist Ettore Sottsass, whom Gastou says is "the Mackintosh of the late 20th century"; and from this time on, he and his wife have been obsessed with contemporary "post-Memphis" creations. On the Gastou dining room table, a Sottsass fruit dish containing a *galette des rois* sits next to a pile of cutouts from Victor's school, bathed in the romantic light of a star-studded Pesce lamp prototype. This is an eccentric but very lively apartment. "If I had had the means," remarks Gastou wistfully, "I would have preferred to hold a competition for contemporary architects, the winner being commissioned to build me a house. As it is, I have to make do with something else."

Comte and Comtesse Hubert d'Ornano live in a luxurious apartment like a world unto itself. "We love living here," says the lady of the house. "I think I prefer entertaining at home to going out." The reception area, with a high ceiling, begins with a broad hallway, off which lies hidden a labyrinth of kitchens, pantries and children's rooms. The three front rooms — salon, dining room and master bedroom — also connect to this hall, forming the heart of an apartment in the classic middle European style. Isabelle d'Ornano is of Polish origin — Potocki on her father's side and Radziwill on her mother's. She decorated her apartment herself, as might be expected, given that she is responsible for styling in the Sisley cosmetics firm, which she co-founded with her husband. She began by remodelling the bare bones of the apartment and altering the ceilings with the advice of Henri Samuel, a highly orthodox decorator. "Ceilings are a vital element of decoration," says Comtesse d'Ornano. "People never pay enough attention to them. I've always been enchanted by the ceilings of Florentine palaces, and I love strong colours. The colour of the *boiseries* in the

RIGHT   *An 18th-century portrait of Barbara Radziwill, a venerated ancestor who was Queen of Poland during the 16th century, hangs in the green salon.*
LEFT   *Detail of Isabelle d'Ornano's bedroom.*
BELOW   *In the dining room the table is covered by a contemporary Persian rug, and dotted with small Meissen figures.*

"I take an instinctive pleasure in Baroque objects, and in things that remind me of my family."
ISABELLE D'ORNANO

A circular mezzanine, used as a dressing room, runs around the entire bedroom, which is decorated in warm-toned fabrics like a boudoir.

salon comes from Versailles. I hate beige and pastel tones generally: reds and greens are what I like."

"Connecting doors should be open at all times, and I wanted the décor to have sufficient continuity to offset the sense of moving from room to room. Also, one should feel at ease in one's own home. My husband is keen on dogs and shooting, so I planned things so that his labradors could come and go without fuss. The house is supposed to revolve around us, rather than vice versa." Thus the four main rooms share the same paisley-patterned carpet, the same quilted furniture and the same houseplants, while their walls tend to be covered with portraits and family photographs. Persian pedestal tables reoccur in room after room, and are also laden with photographs. The pictures record family events, such as the d'Ornanos' visit to Pope John Paul II, as well as Polish ancestors and hunting scenes in the snow. Every room contains hundreds of these images, which are just as likely to be painted by Winterhalter or Serebriakioff as photographed by a child with a shaky hand. Their common denominators are the lives of the Ornano, Potocki and Radziwill families.

As a whole, the decoration of Isabelle d'Ornano's apartment is warm and comfortable, the sort of backdrop one imagines would suit the entourage of Princess Matilda or certain scenes from Visconti's films. This type of international, almost nostalgic ambience, immortalized by 19th-century watercolours, is what Isabelle d'Ornano describes as a *doux fouillis* (charming muddle).

130

"I love roof light; it makes me
feel like I don't quite know where I am,
and it is not necessarily in Paris."
PATRICK CHAUVEAU

Patrick Chauveau lives in a little paved cul-de-sac that runs up against Père Lachaise cemetery, on the east side of the Bastille quarter. This is an area full of paper factories, fabric wholesalers and printers; lately it has attracted painters, sculptors and other artists, who have moved into its unoccupied industrial buildings. The small gardens and ash trees that characterize this decaying quarter of Paris give it a semi-rural air, which adds to its charm. Films are frequently shot here, painters' works are exhibited, parties are held and trucks are constantly being loaded and unloaded.... Patrick Chauveau came to the area because he needed space. Operating with his own craftsmen, he builds sets for the advertising industry and the movies, as well as backgrounds for fashion photographs. Most of his work is done at the last moment, by day or night, to the accompaniment of music. Recently, Chauveau has launched into a parallel career as a painter and sculptor, his main themes deriving from childhood memories. All this is done in a pair of large two-storey buildings, originally used as an engine factory, and

FAR LEFT *Patrick Chauveau's factory gives onto a busy cul-de-sac close to the Père Lachaise cemetery.*
ABOVE *The kitchen in the old factory offices has not been altered.*
LEFT *The workshop area, which is lit from above.*

then converted for the mass production of haberdashery. The former management offices were on the first floor, overlooking the workshops, and it is here that Chauveau has set up house. The area is lit by two small windows overlooking the cul-de-sac, and by an enormous glass roof which illuminates the entire premises. Chauveau can keep an eye on what's going on in his atelier through the internal windows which close off his area. "Plenty of people come by during the day," he says, "people who live or work on the street, friends and artisans, but also the models, stylists and photographers who use my studios. My son is a musician; he sometimes comes here to practise with his group, the 'Soucoupes Violentes.' It's exciting to feel all this life going on around me. The quieter it is, the less productive I am as an artist, but when it's all happening, I can work in here for three days solid: I don't need anything else at all. I feel like I'm the focal point of a small village."

Patrick Chauveau never looks out of his window. "I get easily distracted by whatever's going on outside. I lose my concentration." His living space is entirely closed off to the world; it faces inward, or to the sky, and includes almost no partitions. He sleeps on a mezzanine directly under the roof, on a third level he reaches by a ladder. This ladder is for his private use alone. "Here, I can oversee everything, and this is the most protected place in the building. I don't want to be visited, and no one else has any reason to come in."

The rest of the apartment is made up of a living room.

LEFT *The living area, where Patrick Chauveau paints and sculpts. The ladder leads to his sleeping quarters under the roof.*
RIGHT *Detail of the original partition, now separating the living area and the kitchen.*

136

Chauveau maintains that the reigning disorder in this area is "more creative than one might think." Although he professes to dream of "bright, empty spaces," he is in fact resigned to these bohemian surroundings. On each side of this huge living room, he has converted the old management and accounts departments into a bathroom and a kitchen. Both are chaotic but very clean. And there are plenty of other unconventional touches like the deliberately preserved crumbling wall surface around the basin. As for kitchens, "a kitchen should be practical and rational," says Chauveau. "All I want are things that work...." Nonetheless, Chauveau doesn't rule out the idea of picking up objects on the street or in junkyards.

The door between workshop and living quarters is kept permanently open; thus a kind of flow is established at meals, which are taken with people working on the premises. Equally, there are periods of solitude and introspection when no work is under way. In either case Chauveau occupies his private area like the captain of a ship, in the knowledge that it is part of a larger entity. His home is his personal toy, and its contents emphasize this. The military parachute which serves as a curtain, the Vuitton trunk and the ventilator fans seem to be chosen at random, but they have one thing in common — Chauveau's adherence to a particular style of marginality.

LEFT *The kitchen's decaying look has been carefully preserved, although it is kept immaculately clean.*
RIGHT *An old Vuitton trunk outside the kitchen is indicative of the owner's tastes.*

Pascal Greggory, the actor, belongs to the world of Rohmer and Kleist. His friends include Patrice Chéreau, Nathalie Sarraute, François-Marie Banier and Jacques Grange, whom he requested to "take care of" (not "decorate") this, his first Paris apartment. "I know Jacques' style very well," says Greggory.

"I wanted fewer objects than he has in his house and white walls — a bachelor flat."

"He was very perturbed," recalls Jacques Grange with a smile. "I invented a greyish-white, Paris-roof colour for the place, and I made a special point about his mezzanine, which opens onto a little terrace area. That's where we installed the television, the video, the music and the telephone. He's always up there reading. My main contribution is the bleached oak stairway."

Greggory's loft apartment consists of a huge split-level area with a high ceiling, subdivided into smaller areas with plate-glass windows. Outside, the grey roofs of Paris seem bathed in the light of Rome. Here, in this secluded Saint-Sulpice apartment, the watchwords are friendship and affection. On the same floor as Greggory there lives a movie director, and in the building next door lives a writer. The place is one of worn stairways, locked doors, connecting rooms, people staying and people just dropping in. The residents are secretive and highly civilized, with a dash of the *enfant terrible*: they know how to share a *valet de chambre* and

139

ABOVE   *A Russian chair, a mask by Picasso and a bust of a Greek god sit in the salon before a window offering a view of Saint-Sulpice.*
LEFT   *In the salon a blend of Oriental colours and materials strengthens the impression of warmth and quiet.*

"*This is the first house I ever had, and I think it'll do for the rest of my life.*"
PASCAL GREGGORY

141

maintain an almost classical unity of front and tone, even though Pascal Greggory himself is a ferociously private person. "Very few people come to my house," he says. "I have few friends: about ten, I should think. If I have to talk about work, or if I want to see theatre people, I go somewhere else. This place is my refuge from my bohemian existence." Greggory seldom buys things. "I like large objects," he declares, "massive furniture like the chairs by Frank, Prinz and Muller, made with big lion's feet. And I love curios like my ancient Chinese tree root. But these things don't exclude childish toys such as my robots and my elephants; to me, they are points of reference, just as my books are. In my eyes, these objects are rarities, even though one has no idea of their real value."

LEFT   *The salon, which connects with the mezzanine.*
BELOW   *The mezzanine is almost entirely occupied by a large couch known as a* radassière, *and opens onto a small terrace.*
ABOVE LEFT   *The library, with its oak ceiling, leads to a tiny kitchen.*
ABOVE RIGHT   *Part of Greggory's eclectic collection of chairs.*

"I don't really care for furniture per se. I think it amounts to a flaunting of wealth."
AGNÈS ROSENSTIEHL

Agnès and Pierre Rosenstiehl live on the edge of the Bois de Vincennes. He is a mathematician and she writes children's books and is engaged in a study of Rimbaud's works. Between them they have seven children, from several marriages, who specialize in music, photography, painting, comic-strip art and philosophy. Some still live at home, and the youngest, who is 15, is fond of roller-skating in the kitchen. This creative family has built up its own unconventional atmosphere, in a home that opens onto a wild garden full of stray cats. Here and there in the wasteland are antique statues brought home from the

many trips which have supplied the evolving décor of the house. "Our things arrive in waves, and each new wave takes the place of the one before," says Agnès. "At present, the house is Moroccan, with a strong Rimbaud overlay. We also have some Italian leftovers here and there, along with one or two Finnish touches."

The Rosenstiehl family came to this traditional suburban house about 15 years ago. Their first move was to alter the main staircase, which, Agnès explains, "blocked out the sunshine." Next they painted everything white and knocked down most of the partitions. The ground floor now consists of two large rooms, — the kitchen and library. A large

round table with sturdy chairs, a few shelves, a typewriter, a red-painted piano and plenty of green light filtering through bamboos are now the central decorative features of the main room, which is otherwise focused on a painting by Marie-Thérèse Lanoa, Agnès Rosenstiehl's grandmother. The library is bursting with books. Agnès claims that the population increases at the rate of one per day. "I write, draw

ABOVE LEFT *An American patchwork quilt and early 20th-century paintings by Lanoa adorn the master bedroom overlooking the garden.*
ABOVE RIGHT *The bathroom.*
LEFT *An antique statue stands in the garden.* RIGHT *The street entrance sometimes attracts would-be purchasers who wonder if the house is inhabited.*

and telephone in here," she adds. "Pierre uses the room when he invites his colleagues over, and the children come here to consult the encyclopedias." The two rooms, which connect, are designed for parties of up to 100 people that take place three times a year, as well as for various birthdays and other celebrations involving friends and relatives of all ages. "Everyone's expected to dress up and generally comply with the family's rituals."

The first floor and the attic are divided up into tiny bedrooms with a minimum of furniture — chaotic but very clean.

"I operate along monastic lines," says Agnès ironically. "We have tiny individual cells and huge collective areas. Pierre wants things to be clean and often has the place repainted. He converted me to the colour green, which adds freshness to the atmosphere.

Before we met, I had lived in blue surroundings, to which I added red touches as a matter of principle."

The bathroom is probably the best indicator of the prevailing philosophy here. The space is cluttered with drying laundry and socks draped over radiators, while from the ceiling hangs an elegant but incongruous crystal chandelier. The bath tub, with its lion's feet, stands in the centre of the room opposite a small marble fireplace, which is used in the winter. The two washbasins, of different heights, are faced with ceramic tiles made by Agnès's mother. A lifesize nude of Professor Rosenstiehl as Pythagoras hangs on the wall; this was painted by his father-in-law for the subject's memorable 50th birthday party. On the plinth, the mathematical formula invented by the professor is written in Greek letters.

LEFT AND ABOVE *The library is used by all the family, who take it in turns to work or make music.*
PREVIOUS PAGE *Detail of the chimneypiece, a homage to Rimbaud.*

ABOVE *The entrance, with walls covered by bookshelves. The same cabochon-patterned carpet provides continuity in all the reception rooms.*
LEFT *Detail of the 17th- and 18th-century drawings above the Louis XV table.*
BELOW *The yellow salon, with its moire-covered walls, is 18th century in inspiration.*

"The 18th century saw Western culture at its zenith. The 19th century spoiled everything; it was a cornershop epoch." MANUEL CANOVAS

Manuel Canovas is the only fabric printer ever to have shown his work at the Salon des Arts Decoratifs. This is because his *barré* and flowered motifs are all his own work. Canovas is a great lover of colour, perhaps on account of his Spanish origins; in any event, this taste has been honed by many trips to Mexico and elsewhere. With his wife, Catherine, and his children, he lives beside the Eiffel Tower in a two-floor apartment, which

he chose because of its high ceilings. "In Paris," says Canovas, "the ultimate luxury is plenty of space above one's head!"

The apartment is decorated in pure 18th-century style, doubtless nourished by its owner's memories of his family in Spain. Canovas likes his *lampas* and the damask on his *bergères* to be bright and vivid; and he makes sure that the colours of his *trompe l'œil* marbles sparkle with life. His salon is in yellow watered silk, his dining room is pink, and all the other rooms are

ABOVE *Cool, fresh fabrics have been used in the bedroom of Victoire, aged 9.*
TOP *In the dining room the colours of the table have been chosen to go with the old Sèvres pattern plate.*
RIGHT *The furniture in Catherine Canovas's small boudoir is upholstered in* Bien aimé *fabrics, which complement the "Belem" pattern on the walls. The table is contemporary American.*

upholstered in fabrics with broad designs. The Canovas style is lively, with a hint of the lavish. The architecture of his building has made it possible for him to isolate the "reception" area from the living quarters. Catherine Canovas is especially fond of her dining room, with its bouquets, urns and dried flowers. She is also attached to the tiny office and boudoir, with its pink peony motif, where she oversees her children's homework and sometimes watches television with them. The monumental entrance belies this little suite of private rooms on either side of the main staircase.

In keeping with the English country house style he favours, Canovas's library is filled from floor to ceiling with books, some of which can only be reached by ladders and catwalks. From here, profiled double doors lead to the salon and main dining room, in which hang, Venetian-style, portraits of Canovas's Spanish forebears. The salon is drenched with light; its walls are covered with sepia, red chalk and bister drawings, some by Blas Canovas, the designer's father. There are also a number of paintings collected by an Austrian ancestor, who "refused to buy anything by a Frenchman on account of Napoléon, whom he considered to be the hooligan of Europe." Here Canovas has juxtaposed an Amazon Indian headdress made of feathers with 18th-century Niderwiller wine coolers. The carpet, the same in all three reception rooms, is one of his own designs — pale yellow, with brightly-coloured *cabochons*. This is the only resolutely modern touch in a home which revolves around the objects and ethos of an earlier epoch.

"I wasn't given any choice in the matter. As soon as I showed Andrée Putman the place where I was thinking of setting up my publishing house, she just said 'Leave it to me.' We're very good friends, and on top of that she won me over with an incredibly reasonable quote!"

José Alvarez spends his life in his office, from 9am to 11pm every day. If he isn't there, he's travelling on business. "I can sleep in a cupboard; a bed and a bath are the only things I need."

Les Éditions du Regard, Alvarez's publishing house, is celebrating its eighth year of existence with a series of Russian books on art and theatre. The company operates from a large apartment near the Place des Victoires, with a grey-and-black reception room, a counter and a succession of shelves stacked with the books Alvarez has published.

The boss's grey felt hat and pigskin gloves await him on a Mallet-Stevens chair, along with a copy of *Libération*. The blind is made of metal (this combination of chair and blind has become one of the symbols of the 1980's). A small cat plays among some empty cardboard boxes beside a huge coloured sculpture by Come Mosta-Heirt.

So begins this extraordinary office, which takes up the left-hand side of the apartment. First comes a series of cubbyholes in which Alvarez's colleagues type, pore over proofs and receive authors. This area is black, grey and white, uncluttered like the rest of the apartment, and enlivened by contemporary sculptures and paintings. "My style is based on understatement," says Andrée

LEFT *Two paintings by Stanislas Leplé.*
BELOW *The cat, a gift from Andrée Putman, lies on a chair covered with Russian leather.*
RIGHT *The entrance, with metal blinds and Mallet-Stevens chairs.*

"The only objects I really need are books and paintings."
JOSÉ ALVAREZ

Putman. "I hate to shock." Beyond is José Alvarez's long office, with its staircase leading to a small library-cum-dining room, used for entertaining friends, authors and various partners. This sunlit duplex, which overlooks a modest courtyard, is conceived like a small private apartment, full of books. There is a lingering scent of champagne, flowers and cigars, and the feeling of a real home permeated by undertones of conversation and the comings and goings of the artists with whom Alvarez's books are mainly concerned. In May 1988, Éditions du Regard published a huge volume on Jean-Pierre Raynaud, who brought in a huge flowerpot covered in gold leaf by way of thanks.

"I love office life," confesses Alvarez. "I'm incapable of reading in bed or even of staying there very long. The only place I can work is behind my table — furthermore, the table is just about the only piece of furniture that interests me. I chose this one myself; it looks completely anonymous, but it came from the 1937 art déco exhibition in Paris. Otherwise, the only objects I really need are books, paintings by artists like Degottex and Wabi and, oddly enough, the things one uses at table. Furniture leaves me completely cold. I may have plenty of ideas about clothes, but as far as décor is concerned I have none at all. Andrée took care of everything, in particular the interior architectural work. She knows what I like. The green carpeting was her idea; I thought at first it looked a bit staid, but now I've become fond of it. The *chaise-longue* was also a Putman brainwave. She thought it might tempt me to take a rest from time to time, but I don't leave my table nowadays any more than I did before."

LEFT AND BELOW LEFT *José Alvarez's office with the staircase leading to the dining room.*
BELOW RIGHT AND RIGHT *The pattern of the 19th-century tableware reflects the grey-and-black tiled table, which is bedecked with a bottle of Moët and Chandon, asparagus and friesias in soliflores created by Andrée Putman.*

"Fine architecture and beautiful objects are fine; but I dislike 'decoration' for its own sake."
HUGO DUJOUR

Riesener, Oebe and Séné have no secrets for Hugo Dujour, a young art historian with a taste for 18th-century French furniture. This is why he jokingly claims that he pays more attention to his collections of drawings, paintings and Lorraine pottery than to his furniture, which will never be beautiful enough for his taste.
The building in which he lives is solid and comfortable, near

the Musée d'Orsay. He came here because the architecture allowed him to hang his 17th-century Flemish tapestry. The tapestry features a landscape framed by flowers and cupids, in which a warlike female brandishes a blue crab, symbolizing the astrological sign of Cancer. This character creates the ambience of the garnet-red salon, which is complemented by the green tones of the bedroom.
"I know I should have put that tapestry on damask, but I didn't like the shiny, rather

sumptuous appearance of the fabric. I went to Laurent Potoniée for advice and we had a crimped faille specially woven and dyed. The result is much more matt, not unlike brocatelle." To illustrate, Dujour opens an armoire bursting with fabric samples: lampas, damask, satin, brocades and brocatelles. "I

ABOVE   *An 18th-century Lorraine terracotta in the bedroom.*
RIGHT   *In the salon the Flemish tapestry, which measures 21 × 12 ft, entirely covers the walls of the room. The Smyrna rug seems to prolong its effect.*

wanted to recreate a 19th-century Mario Praz type of ambience, and I followed the theory of never trying to achieve a 19th-century effect with 19th-century objects. Hence the upholstered chairs juxtaposed with 18th-century seats and secretaires. The chairs are only important as comfortable places to sit and anyway, I've always been partial to English houses where one can be comfortable even though surrounded by beautiful things. In France we always seem to have fragile chairs and precarious spidery tables right in the middle of the room. As far as I'm concerned, this is rather like a furniture warehouse, in which I happen to work and sleep." The green room, the walls of which are stretched with sateen, echoes the intimate, muted quality of the salon. "I work in every room in the house,"

confesses Hugo, who has turned the apartment's octagonal dining room into a bedroom crammed with books. Files, newspapers, samples, catalogues, scarves, hammers and the inevitable books lie about everywhere; one expects at any moment to fall over a decrepit dog. This bohemian atmosphere contrasts strongly with the beauty of the collections, imparting an irresistible sense of liveliness to the space. Corridors with odd corners still covered with dingy wallpaper lead through a tiny kitchen to further oddities at the far end of the apartment, but the entrance itself is resolutely serious. "I see it as the hall of a private collector's house," Dujour continues. The floor is covered with a pattern of black and white *cabochons*, and the other space is taken up by *trompe l'œil* marble and Russian leather chairs. In short,

it is elegant, orthodox and Parisian.

Hugo mostly works at home and seldom entertains, but this does not prevent him from improvising fried eggs for visitors, or running round to a *patisserie* for other provisions. On such occasions, plates and cake-boxes invade his brocaded chairs and Smyrna rugs. While looking ruminatively at the lady with the blue crab, Hugo wonders if she approves of the way he lives and surmises that he'll never know for certain.

ABOVE   *The octagonal bedroom with its broad Empire bookcases. The blinds are kept permanently shut.*
RIGHT   *The bathroom is hidden behind an old-fashioned cretonne in a passage leading to the bedroom.*

To find the photographers Pierre et Gilles, you have to follow the trail of dusted gold paint which leads up the staircase to the Bastille garrets where they live and work. At the entrance, you hear the twittering of the birds that live in the artificial trees. Pierre and Gilles dislike the word "kitsch" when applied to their work or their apartment, but with the best will in the world it is hard to avoid. They want no truck with the past — "We don't like old things and we never go to the fleamarket" — nor do they take kindly to mockery. They're thoroughly modern — their culture is post-1968, essentially musical and *populaire*.

Gilles Blanchard attended the Beaux-Arts, while Pierre Commoy studied photography. They met in 1974, and their shared style is the result of that meeting. Their work mainly consists of record covers (for Lio, Etienne Daho and Mikado, among other French stars), magazine covers (*Marie Claire, Zoom, Actuel*) and exhibition pieces (Musée d'Art Moderne, Galerie Samis, Saouma). When we visited Pierre and Gilles, they were busy with a book for Éditions du Contrejour, to appear at the end of 1988; they were also involved in making video clips for two rock groups. They are nothing if not highly professional and perfectionist, and their ikons are very eclectic. They include Tarzan, Snow White and the Seven Dwarfs, St. Teresa, Claude François, Sheila, Madonna, Sylvie Vartan, Michael Jackson, Barbie dolls, teddy bears and their parakeets, Pouet-Pouet and Bibique (originally found bedraggled and starving under a *porte cochère*). All are "cultural" elements that reoccur in their sets and in their apartment, which has to be one of the most joyous and youthful to be found in Paris. The Japanese, in particular, are great lovers of their work, but when they go abroad, Pierre and Gilles tend to head for India, Turkey, Morocco or Santo Domingo. They love the East. "But wherever we happen to be," they explain, "we avoid castles and famous monuments like the plague. On the contrary, we aim straight for the working-class areas, where we seek out the bazaars. The things we buy are never expensive, but that isn't intentional."

Pierre and Gilles are simple, serious and gentle to a fault. Their apartment is like they are, tranquil and welcoming; there is no hallway, one walks straight into the living room. The windows are veiled by Indian flowered curtains, doubled by fishnets hung with starfish. On the windowsills are plastic toys like those to be found in children's sandpits : fish, turtles and inflatable rabbits. A large, much-used colour television stands in the

LEFT *The letterbox at the bottom of the stairs.*
RIGHT *Pierre and Gilles often have their portraits done by local artists when they travel.*

"*We love bazaars, working-class districts and cheap goods. Our style, such as it is, comes from our travels.*"
PIERRE AND GILLES

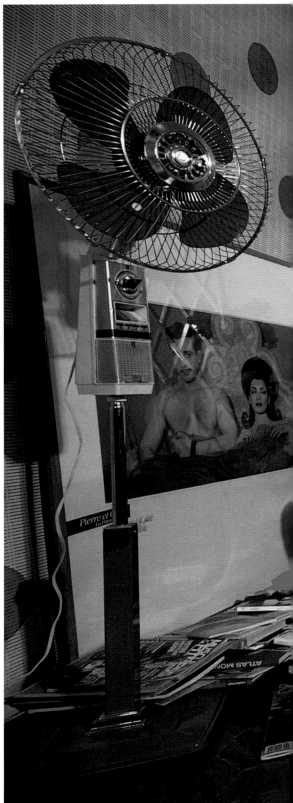

Two views of the living room. On the left, on the television screen, a frame from a video by Pierre and Gilles. Other videos wait in suitcases found in the Arab quarter of Marseille. Above the corner sofa facing the television.

corner between two North African suitcases, painted and filled with cassettes; on top of the television is an assortment of artificial flowers and Indian divinities. The centre of the room is occupied by a large, convivial table, set with plastic utensils "chosen for their form or colour," like the magisterial Arab coffee pot.

Since Pierre and Gilles maintain a certain ritual in their lives, and like to entertain their friends in reasonable style, the living room also contains a sofa which was "found on the street" and is now surrounded by Smurf toy figures.

The tiny blue-painted bedroom has a single dormer window overlooking the courtyard. The bed, with its Turkish cover, occupies almost the entire space. Pierre's panther-spotted dressing gown hangs on a coat rack, while Gilles's Arab slippers await him at the end of the bed. There's scarcely room at the head for the electric bouquet of red roses that serves as a lamp, or for the alarm clock from Mecca that commands the pair to begin the day "with rooster, running water and verses from the Koran." They found this object in Montmartre; many of their other knicknacks came from Brussels, where there is a large Turkish community. Pouet-Pouet often perches on Pierre's shoulder while he talks. Meanwhile Gilles is busy making coffee in the kitchen and, on the television screen, Mikado is singing *La fille du soleil* in a two-piece bathing suit.

TOP *The living room's large convivial table.* ABOVE *Detail of table showing the pet birds Pouet-Pouet and Bibique at liberty.* RIGHT *The bedroom, dominated by a picture of Claude François, framed with white roses.*

> *"I would prefer to hire a very expensive carpenter to do a job people will scarcely notice than to spend the same money accumulating valuable objects."*
> *JACQUES GRANGE*

Jacques Grange is the decorator of the hour. His clients include Lloyds of London, the Musée de la Mode in Paris, Paloma Picasso, Yves Saint Laurent and Isabelle Adjani. Even Catherine Deneuve comes to him for advice. He is the current darling of the French bourgeoisie because he has created a muted, discreet style with the merit of banishing visible signs of wealth. Jacques Grange has two houses. His public "success" home is Colette's former residence on the Palais-Royal, and it is here that he gives parties. His private home is the same duplex on the Luxembourg Gardens in which he has lived from the beginning, and in which he still spends most of his time. The décor here was completed in 1970 and has

had time to acquire the patina of use and age; it illustrates a number of Grange's principles, which have changed little in the intervening years. Grange, with his perpetual scarf and dufflecoat, still possesses the modesty of an adolescent. He willingly acknowledges his masters: after attending the Boulle and Camondo school, he learned *"passementerie, boiserie* and the French tradition of precision and quality" from Henri Samuel. Later, he worked with Jean Demachy for several years, where he met talented individuals like Madeleine Castaing. But the great influence in his life, the house he still refers to as a yardstick, was that of Marie-Laure de Noailles at Hyères, designed by Mallet Stevens. "Her view of the world marked me for life," explains Grange.

"I was just over 20 when I met Marie-Laure and I was stunned by her way of mixing valuable objects with the things she happened to be fond of at a given moment. Her house was a work of art, conceived by a great architect, and it served her own special *art de vivre*. The people there, and the things that happened there, were just as important as the objects. It was a complete creation, and it hugely influenced my work; it made me understand that apartments are not for looking at but for living in. What counts most for me is that things should be natural and expressive of well-being... but how does one

ABOVE *The charm of an antiquated courtyard: no elevator and no code to open the door.*
LEFT *The entrance hall, with cool linen curtains and a narrow Chinese-style staircase.*

168

achieve that? The book within reach, good lighting, a beckoning armchair."

"I also try to adapt to the space I am working on. There's a relationship between a place and its decoration which must be respected. I would never attempt to fit Louis XV *boiseries* into a loft apartment. My collaboration with Yves Saint Laurent, which was a dual creative effort, is the perfect case in point: I had to begin with a small, modernist studio, followed by an Orientalist villa in Marrakech and a Visconti-style house in Deauville. On the face of it, none of these projects had anything in common."

In Grange's loft on the Luxembourg Gardens, the entry hall offers a foretaste of what is to come. The smallness of the room is counteracted by a looking glass which covers an entire wall. The kilim-covered cushions on the radiator seem braced to receive a cat, while the window is half-veiled by a freshly starched linen curtain. Everything here seems calculated to evoke the *bonne maison* of provincial France, an older Europe stolidly unmoved by success. On this floor, the ceilings are very low,

and the salon-cum-library-cum-dining room has been distempered with a kind of tavern brown (ceiling included). A fire crackles in the grate, and lines of books run around the room in specially made wire-fronted cabinets. But, strangely, Michel Leiris, Raymond Queneau, Pierre Loti, F. M. Banier and Marcel Proust are kept under lock and key. "I read too little these days," laments Jacques Grange. "When I decorated this apartment, I was trying for the exposed-beam, Left Bank look." And, he adds, whenever he visits his friend Yves Saint Laurent in Morocco, he always takes along *Thousand and One Nights.*

The books, the brick-coloured 1900 rug laid over the carpet, the kilims and plush on the chairs, all look irresistibly comfortable. Tones of a worn red-brown lead in a succession of nuances to a bouquet of "Tango" roses which sets off the faded, lived-in atmosphere of the room. Jacques Grange dislikes bright colours, and the grey-green look of the pine bookcases and the white oak have as much value here as a turquoise green or peacock blue at Madeleine Castaing's house.

On the second level of the apartment is an atelier with a high skylight; this room connects to the bedroom and bathroom. Below, it was winter; here, it's summer. The atmosphere is all white — white blinds, white walls; green houseplants add a colonial touch. Somehow this is reminiscent of the Musée des Arts Africains at the Porte Dorée: plaster "black boys," assorted travel souvenirs, banana wood and boxwood furniture, Egyptian stools and silhouettes from the 1930's, the ensemble distributed under a benign tropical fan. If Princess Margaret never played the bakelite piano in the entrance, she certainly used one exactly like it. This is Grange's nostalgia room, completed by a large rug with a giant motif that recalls Matisse or even Madame Butterfly.

The J. M. Frank lamp was a gift from Aragon; in the bedroom the tulips came from Madeleine Castaing and the golden apple from Claude Lalanne. Jacques Grange has many photographs of friends, which reveal a tender side to his nature. The same quality appears in the 1905 Bonnard-style screen (mounted by Majorelle), which reminds him of pictures in books he read as a child, as does his Jules Verne metal bedside lamp.

The bathroom is functional without seeming to be, with its capacious Russian verandah armchair. The bathtub is framed by peculiar ceramics and the basin is set into an old faïence stove. Here, as elsewhere in the house, the tone is one of nonchalant sensuality, backed by solid but discreet *savoir-faire.* The mirrors are effective but not obvious, and the closets are present but practically invisible. This complicated apartment, with its unequal spaces, cast-iron spiral staircase, courtyard with ivy-covered statues, floor tiles on the landing and worn oak steps, is the *pied-à-terre* of Jacques Grange's personal dream. It is the kind of priceless, marvellous hideout that gives Paris, and more especially the Left Bank, its eternal magical quality.

172

"I know my monkeys, my barbotines and my vanités *worry other people, but for me they represent pure fantasy."* MONY LINTZ EINSTEIN

Mony Lintz Einstein lives in a ground-floor apartment behind a high wall in Saint-Germain-des-Prés. The shutters are grey in the French style, and the windows look onto a garden filled with white flowers. Light floods into the house, and the green of the foliage complements the colours of the décor. Everything is calm and harmonious, although the apartment's eccentric owner has created an atmosphere

here that can only be described as esoteric. First of all, objects abound on floors and walls, and there is little furniture. The disorder is carefully calculated, a "jumble" she calls it, and the effect is not unlike a still life by Salvador Dali. Mony Lintz Einstein's mother was obsessed by "clinical" order, and her family counts one of mankind's greatest geniuses among its members. Perhaps her taste for the extraordinary is inherited but, in any event, everything in Mony's house is "out of sync." Style and value are secondary

considerations for her. Hence a statue by Salvador Dali stands beside a set of fake mushrooms, Bavarian hunting-lodge furniture and bistro chairs. All this is part of a definite mental approach to the world. After studying literature, Mony became a picture dealer, and she is still fascinated by contemporary painting. Her life was given a new direction after a trip to India, where she developed a passion (now outgrown) for beaten silver furniture. This led her to change professions and become an antique dealer, and her

shop, Epoqua, has now been operating for over 12 years. "The main room of my house should be a place of constant amusement both for me and for other people," she explains. "Objects come and go but I always try to maintain an aquatic, plant-filled atmosphere — thus, my passion for *barbotines*, (19th-century French ceramicware known for its relief representation of plants and animals and its colours). I'm sure this is linked to something deep in my unconscious. I also collect shells, rocks, grotto furniture

Tulips at tea-time, featuring a "Brindille" tea service, a chair made of elk and Bavarian stag antlers, and a timeless Saint Bernard of the 1830's.

and *vanités*, those 17th-century paintings that contain objects evoking the senses. I love my collection of monkeys in wood, porcelain and bronze. All these things evoke nature and are in harmony with the house's exterior."

The entrance is somewhat gloomy, permanently stacked with objects in transit. It leads to a small office, decorated with what Mony calls a "masculine" cashmere pattern, it contains a fireplace and an old Chesterfield sofa. Next comes a long room decorated with false marble, which opens onto the garden. On the salon side there is a central divan of multi-coloured pouffes, with billowing tulle and the occasional porcelain hand poking weirdly out of the fabric. The overall effect is of a sleeping Gorgon. Mony is intensely enthusiastic and mercurial, always trying to catch up on some treasured project or dream. She uses her private "bestiary" to test, captivate and amuse her guests; hers is a mysterious world, where ceramic eels slither through ferns, monkeys wear embroidered waistcoats and fruit, vegetables, marble and dogs are all false. All the same, Mony's objects are chosen for their beauty more than for their strangeness: they are never provocative, kitsch or malign. The apartment would be comfortable, intimate and even bourgeois were it not for the sense of interrogation that the décor imparts. Finally, the bedroom, "which other people's eyes must never see," is where Mony goes to escape the strange magic she has worked.

174

ABOVE Barbotines, monkeys, skulls and a Guatemalan stirrup in a corner of the salon.
TOP AND RIGHT Indian and Bavarian chairs surround an Indian table, with pastries on Chinese plates, fake cherries
and an 18th-century biscuitware cock next to 1950's Murano glasses.

Loulou de la Falaise's huge atelier in the XIVth *arrondissement* exudes an atmosphere of ease and illusion. Nothing here is precious, but everything is elegant. Loulou is the right hand and muse of Yves Saint Laurent, and specializes in jewelry design. Her writer husband, Thadée Klossowski (son of Balthus), likes to say he does nothing, even though he has studied Georges Bataille for many years and is currently completing a voluminous study of the contemporary novel. The atelier smells of freshly-ironed linen, and the atmosphere owes much to ample 1930's proportions. Because the ceiling is so high, Loulou and Thadée have been able to hang an immense chandelier from its centre; this piece, which originally came from the Hotel Claridge in Paris, is lit only with candles. Beneath the chandelier is an equally extravagant bed that looks like it came from a Venetian palace. The carpet is midnight blue, the colour which dominates the apartment.

LEFT   *The Klossowskis occupy two artists' studios in a 1930's building.*
RIGHT   *Detail of the salon, with a portrait of Maxime de la Falaise, Loulou's mother, as a child, and in front of it the crown Loulou wore to the "Fairy Ball" at the Hôtel Lambert.*

"My mother sent this American-Baroque-Louis XV bed across from New York...."
LOULOU DE LA FALAISE

OVERLEAF   *A huge chandelier hangs over a Baroque bed in the salon. In the foreground a Schiaparelli pipe lies under a bronze by Sheridan of Loulou's father, Alain de la Falaise, which has a theatrical crown on top.*

178

Loulou's fabrics are mostly old: indigo ikats and faded silks. The mezzanine above serves as the couple's bedroom, and from the loggia hangs a collection of Indonesian batiks made at the turn of the century. Both above and below, the curtains are white, fresh and billowing. Some run along the walls on rods, evoking the atmosphere of a couture house: an impression heightened by the odd tulle or satin dress Loulou leaves about.

There are books everywhere, ranging from Rilke to *Babar en Famille*. The rule of the house is that nothing should seem too serious; thus the crown Loulou wore recently to a "fairy ball" was curiously similar to the one perched rakishly on a bronze Sheridan bust of her father. The least ray of sunshine creates a twinkling in the crystal chandelier and a glimmering in the gilt; and when night falls, the room blazes with light from the hundred reflected candles. A party could break out at any moment.

RIGHT   *The bedroom on the mezzanine with its voluminous white cotton curtains.*
BELOW   *Looking up to the mezzanine, where Loulou's collection of blue Indonesian batiks, dating from the early 20th century, hangs from the balustrade.*

AFTERWORD

The Countess d'Ornano; a retired working woman in the *quartier populaire* of Belleville; a writer entrenched off the Faubourg St. Germain; an artist living way up in the 13th arrondissement . . . what do all the people in this book have in common?

The answer: they are Parisians, and unlike many of their kind in the late 20th century, they are Parisians who view their homes with special fondness and respect. Each has designed and decorated his or her abode in an entirely individual way, often according to very nontraditional principles.

The compilation of this book has raised problems of tolerance, and above all, of taste. Isabelle d'Ornano defines this elusive quality as "a tiny spark within one, which reveals things that other people cannot see." Jean-Louis Gaillemin, editor-in-chief of the French magazine *L'Objet d'Art*, wonders if taste exists at all, adding that if it does "it is poles apart from what we call 'good taste'; what I am talking about is a purely personal thing."

Andrée Putman, a personification of 1980s modernity, believes that taste is closely associated with strength of character "because if the fantasy that governs one's arrangement of things is not absolutely sincere, one gets nowhere at all; in other words one achieves nothing but a measure of comfort and equilibrium."

"One must simply be inspired," declares Madeleine Castaing, at the age of 94 still the queen of Parisian decoration. Yet Mme. Castaing has never succeeded in eclipsing the memory of Marie-Laure de Noailles, whose name crops up unfailingly wherever the magic of houses is a topic of conversation.

To my mind, harmony is a more important element than taste. Harmony is born of the mysterious union between an individual and his ability to express his deepest fantasies, his obsessions, his secret adventures and voyages, using the vehicles of volume, color, matter, and objects. "I am convinced that one must be thoroughly excited by a set of objects if one is ever to assemble them successfully," asserts Andrée Putman.

Alas, examples of such sincere dwellings are few and far between, and all too often one's most memorable evenings and conversations in Paris take place amid visually dull surroundings. Most apartments obey standard rules laid down by the period, the fashion, the current decorators, in much the same way as dress obeys the stipulations of designers. Thus houses are by Grange, Mongiardino, Catroux, Badin, or Walbaum, just as clothes are by Saint Laurent, Lacroix, Yamamoto, or Agnès B. On the other hand, the Bastille area scarcely bestows the same social cachet as the Faubourg St. Germain or the lower 12th arrondissement; consequently, the possession of a Lalanne sculpture, a Giacometti table, a Garoust and Bonetti "barbarian" lamp, a 1920s Vuitton trunk, or a Mallet-Stevens chair is acknowledged in different ways according to the context.

Hence things are still the same old "things," as analysed by Georges Perec. Things form a network of tiny clues about a person, which Parisians never tire of interpreting. Things pigeonhole a person as elegant, snobbish, hip, marginal, or obscure.

Molière said that as far as he was concerned "there is no refuge for honest people except in Paris," but I prefer Hemingway's pronouncement, "Paris is a party." The city contains a vast spectrum of different but interacting cultures; it also supports a range of expression and statement that can assimilate a Jacob bed, a railway sleeper, a garden allotment, and a bust of Mme. Roland with all the freedom—and all the goodwill—in the world.

Marie-France Boyer